WRITING
BY
WILBERS

Collected Columns: Volume 2

Writing
by
Wilbers

*Entertaining, Helpful Advice
for Everyone Who Writes on the Job*

Stephen Wilbers

The Good Writing Press
Minneapolis

Printed in the United States of America.

First published in 1995.

Library of Congress Catalog Card Number: 95-80022

ISBN: 0-9635995-1-8

The Good Writing Press
4828 Tenth Avenue South
Minneapolis, MN 55417-1163

To you, my readers

Contents

INTRODUCTION
Are Common Errors Undermining Your Credibility? . . 2

A PLAN FOR IMPROVEMENT
New Year's Resolutions for Improving Your Writing . . 6
Faithful Readers at Midpoint in 10-week Exercise 9
Readers Respond to 10-week Writing Challenge 11

MAKING IT SHORT AND SWEET
One MBA Executive's Writing Style: A Critique 14
Send Your Boss to Language Efficiency School 17
Pseudo-sophistication No Justification for Obfuscation . 19

FROM PREWRITING TO POSTWRITING
The Five Elements of Effective Writing 24
To Overcome Writer's Block, Silence Inner Critic 27
Reinstate the Quality Loop To Ensure Good Writing . . 30

BETWEEN YOU AND ME
Wanted: Top-level Managers To Edit Staff Writing . . . 34
Trust Is Key to Cross-racial Writing Criticism 37
Successful Dictation Depends on Collaboration 40

CONNECTING THROUGH CORRESPONDENCE
Sales Letters Succeed by Linking Product to Need 44
Openings Are Key to Successful Sales Letters 47
Dos and Don'ts for Writing Holiday Greetings 49
How To Say, "You're Wrong," Yet Keep Business . . . 52

THE ELECTRONIC REVOLUTION
How Word Processors Help and Hurt Our Writing . . . 56
It's Writer vs. Machine in a Fight over Language 59
Writing with the Word Processor 62
Use the Computer To Help You Think and Write 64

THE ELEMENTS OF SMILE
Humor Can Establish Common Ground with Reader . . . 68
The War of the Words—Invasion of the Bureaucrats . . . 71
Slumberwrite Software "Revolutionizes" Writing 74
Speaking English as it Was Meant To Be Spoken 77
Humor Can Take You Far—Sometimes Too Far 79

TRICKS OF THE TRADE
Five Easy Lessons in Clear Thinking and Writing 84
Writing Can Help You Prepare a Terrific Speech . . . 87
"Elegant Variation" Is an Affectation To Avoid 90
Some Operating Principles that Apply to Writing 93
Verbing Your Nouns and Nouning Your Verbs 96

WRITING ON THE JOB
The Three-step Memo Gets the Job Done in a Pinch . . 100
The Executive Summary and the One-page Report . . . 103
Making Performance Reviews Less of a Burden 106
"Adequate" Not Adequate in Performance Reviews . . 109
How to Make Letters of Recommendation Work 112

DOING IT WITH STYLE!
To Improve Skills, Read (and Copy) Good Writers . . 116
Variety in Sentence Structure Invigorates Writing . . . 119
"How Can I Learn To Write with Style?" 122
Adapt Your Style To Fit the Audience, Occasion 124

THE KUDOS FILE
Touching Letter Offers Reason To Say Thanks 128
Handwritten Notes of Appreciation Create Goodwill . . 130

THE BIG PICTURE
Avoid Errors When Writing Internationally 134
Who Gets the Blame for Illiteracy in America? 137
How Would You Grade Your Business Writing? 140
The Book No Business Writer Should Be Without . . . 143
What Poets Can Teach Us about Using Language . . . 145

WORKS CITED / RECOMMENDED READING . . 150

INDEX 154

x

Introduction

Are Common Writing Errors Undermining Your Credibility?

When I first started writing this column in December 1991, I quoted management expert Peter Drucker, who reminds us, "As soon as you move one step up from the bottom, your effectiveness depends on your ability to reach others through the spoken or written word."

I also quoted author William Zinsser, who makes the point more bluntly: "Bad writing makes bright people look dumb."

Then as now, the purpose of this column is to help make bright people look bright.

You can ensure that your writing reflects the quality of your thinking by doing two things.

First, you can learn and abide by certain principles of good writing (omit needless words, vary your sentence structure and length, lead off with your purpose statement, organize your thought in paragraphs introduced by clear topic sentences, support your arguments with specific examples and illustrations, etc.). As we all know, writing can be a difficult and challenging task, even for the most skillful writers. The *principles* of good writing, however, are simple and straightforward.

Second, you can avoid common writing errors (incorrect punctuation between sentences, misplaced or missing commas, lack of subject/verb agreement, nonparallel constructions, etc.). These errors may undermine your credibility in the eyes of an educated reader.

Here is a simple test to help you assess your writing competence in terms of identifying and avoiding common errors.

The four sentences below illustrate six mistakes in grammar and spelling. Can you spot the errors?

1. "The complexity of the problems make this a difficult issue."

2. "The Good Writing Press may have to trim their payroll, however, the company is expecting new demand for it's products."

3. "Good communication skills can help managers affect change."

4. "Our procedures for following up on delinquent accounts are inconsistent, incomplete, and not reliable."

If you are writing at a level of basic competence, you should readily recognize all six errors. They are:

■Lack of subject/verb agreement (one of the most common grammatical errors in business writing). The first sentence should read: "The complexity of the problems *makes* this a difficult issue." The subject, "complexity," is singular and therefore takes a singular verb, "makes," despite the intervening phrase, "of the problems."

■In the second sentence, the plural pronoun "their" should be singular ("its") so that it agrees in number with its singular antecedent, "The Good Writing Press." When referring to a company, office, division, or agency, be sure to use the singular "it" and "its" rather than the plural "they" and "their."

■The second sentence is a "comma splice" or two independent sentences joined by a comma rather than separated by a period, semicolon, or dash. "However" is an adverb, not a conjunction such as "and" or "but," so it cannot be used to join two independent clauses.

■In the second sentence, the possessive pronoun "its" requires no apostrophe. "It's" is a contraction of "it is."

■"Affect" and "effect" are often misused. "To affect" means "to influence"; "to effect" means "to bring about," as in "to effect change" (which is how the third sentence should read). "Effect" can also be used as a noun, as in "to have an effect on something."

■To maintain parallel structure, the fourth sentence should read "inconsistent, incomplete, and *unreliable*." If you begin a series with a certain part of speech or pattern, you should complete the series in like fashion. Changing the pattern jars the reader. This is particularly important when writing procedures or compiling lists.

A simple self-assessment like this obviously has its limitations. It will tell you little about your ability to organize your thought into coherent paragraphs, for example. It does, however, provide a rough indication of your language skills. If you recognized all six mistakes, you are probably a competent writer. If you identified only one or two errors, you may be writing at a level that undermines or detracts from your credibility.

A Plan for Improvement

New Year's Resolutions for Improving Your Writing

A new year is a time of new beginnings, a time when we take a look at ourselves, our ambitions, our hopes, our expectations—and, of course, our writing skills—and we resolve to make some changes in our lives.

On the outside chance that in making your New Year's resolutions you forgot to include something about improving your ability to communicate, I'm here to help you out.

I have a plan. It will take you anywhere from five minutes to one hour a day and 10 weeks to complete.

To make it easy, I'll provide a list of goals for you to choose from. Pick any 10. (If you're feeling creative, make up a few of your own.)

■Write first drafts without stopping to revise.

■Write at the same time every day.

■Write in stages, allowing your copy to "cool off" between drafts.

■Delete unnecessary words (change "until such time as" to "until" and "due to the fact that" to "because").

■Avoid fancy language ("We need to . . ." rather than "I deem it imperative that we . . .").

■Buy a good dictionary. (I recommend the new edition of the *American Heritage Dictionary*).

■Identify the five words that you misspell most frequently and learn to spell them correctly.

■Make up a list of word pairs that you tend to confuse (such as "affect/effect" and "complement/compliment").

■Make up a list of words you should know in your profession and start using them.

■Use action verbs rather than nominalizations ("I recommend . . ." rather than "My recommendation is . . .").

■Use inclusive language ("Good managers motivate their staff members" rather than "A good manager motivates his staff members").

■Vary your sentence length and sentence structure.

■Write in short sentences and short paragraphs for emphasis.

■Pay particular attention to clarity and tone in openings and closings.

■Place purpose statements in the opening sentence or paragraph (unless you're writing a bad-news letter, in which case open with a buffer).

■Organize paragraphs under clear topic sentences.

■Use transitional words (such as "therefore" and "nevertheless") and transitional phrases (such as "despite these problems" and "for these reasons") to connect your thought between paragraphs.

■Support your arguments with specific and concrete examples.

■Read out loud when editing.

■Make several passes through a document when proofreading, moving from the general to the particular.

■Establish an editing partnership with a colleague.

■Start learning how to type.

■Begin using a word processor.

■Use the spell-check, thesaurus, and grammar-check functions on your word processor (but don't always trust them).

■Read a book for fun and pleasure.

■Mark passages from your on-the-job reading that seem particularly well written.

■Start a file of samples of good writing.

■Copy or type over a document that you think is particularly well written and examine the language.

■Buy a reference book for the office and spend 10 minutes browsing through it. (I recommend Brusaw, Alred, and Oliu's *The Business Writers' Handbook* and Schell and Stratton's *Writing on the Job*.)

■Read a book on principles of composition and style. (I recommend Strunk and White's *The Elements of Style* and William Zinsser's *On Writing Well*).

Have you identified your 10 goals? Good. Now, arrange them in whatever order you like, but I suggest that you begin with the more basic and work your way to the more challenging.

Here's the plan.

Over the next 10 weeks work on accomplishing one goal each week. At the end of 10 weeks, send me a note letting me know how you did.

If you follow your plan, I guarantee that you will be a better writer this year than you were last year. How's that for a resolution?

Faithful Readers at Midpoint
in 10-week Exercise

For those of you working diligently on your New Year's resolution to improve your writing, this is the end of Week 5 of your 10-week plan.

Keep up the good work!

If you have lapsed in your commitment, I urge you to pick up where you left off. Remember: Even if you don't accomplish every one of your goals, whatever you *do* accomplish will probably help you develop your writing skills.

For those of you feeling left out, let me explain.

At the beginning of the year I wrote a column guaranteeing you would be a better writer this year than you were last year if you picked 10 goals for improving your writing and worked on accomplishing one of those goals each week.

To help you devise your plan, I suggested some possible goals, things such as deleting unnecessary words ("until" rather than "until such time as"), avoiding fancy language ("We need to . . ." rather than "I deem it imperative that we . . ."), making up a list of confusing word pairs (such as "affect/effect" and "complement/compliment"), using action verbs rather than nominalizations ("I recommend . . ." rather than "My recommendation is . . ."), using inclusive language ("Good managers motivate their staff members" rather than "A good manager motivates his staff members"), placing purpose statements in your opening sentences or paragraphs (unless you're writing a bad-news letter, in which case you should open with a buffer), etc.

I also invited you to send me a note at the end of your 10-week effort to let me know how things had gone for you.

Apparently, many of you are taking my challenge seriously. Stephanie Slack, a legal secretary from Brooklyn Center, Minn., has already written to tell me that she will try the plan and that she will report her progress to me.

Just to remind you, Ms. Slack, and everyone else who has taken the pledge: *Your report is due to me in five weeks.* No slacking off now.

Another reader, Tom Anderson, a technical writer from White Bear Lake, Minn., wrote to ask a question. He wanted to know how to determine when the word "that" is necessary in a sentence and when it may be omitted.

As an example, Mr. Anderson quoted a sentence from my New Year's column ("If you follow your plan, I guarantee that you will be a better writer this year than you were last year"), and he asked if the sentence would lose any meaning or emphasis if "that" were removed.

The nerve. Correcting a syndicated columnist, a professional writing consultant, a Ph.D., an expert no less. (By the way, I define "expert" as a person who travels more than 30 miles to make a presentation for which he or she is paid more than $10, and I do qualify.)

Actually, it's a good question, one that people ask me frequently. Or should that be "one people ask me frequently"?

The answer is that "that" can be used in numerous ways (as a relative pronoun, a demonstrative pronoun, a conjunction, and even an adverb), but here's a good general rule: "That" may be deleted to pick up the pace or flow of a sentence, unless it is needed for clarity.

In other words, you have the option of writing either "I know that he is bright" or "I know he is bright." But you cannot remove "that" from a sentence such as this one without causing ambiguity: "The attorney believed that her client might jump bail."

As Mr. Anderson rightly suggests, removing "that" from my sentence ("If you follow your plan, I guarantee [that] you will be a better writer this year than you were last year") does improve the sentence stylistically without diminishing its clarity.

But I could still argue that that "that" that that sentence contained was correct.

Readers Respond to 10-week Writing Challenge

Ah, spring. Sweet, sweet spring. It's finally here, that glorious season when ''a livelier iris changes on the burnish'd dove,'' and our fancy lightly turns to thoughts of—you guessed it—writing.

Yes, it's that time of year, a time of rebirth and reawakening, a time when we naturally think back to the dead of winter and we recall all those well-intentioned promises we made as New Year's Resolutions.

I can guess what's on your mind. As the days grow longer, the sun climbs higher in the sky, the ice begins to crack and boom on the lakes, and those last white patches vanish from your front yard, you keep asking yourself: Have I kept my promise to improve my writing this year?

Well, I'm pleased to tell you that you're not alone. In fact, I just received word from Deanna Louie, who teaches English 105 at the Cambridge Community College Campus of Anoka-Ramsey that her entire class took the pledge.

Louie writes: ''Your challenge to your readers to select 10 goals to tackle in 10 weeks gave a real world quality to our work. Students with writing difficulties tend to think no one has writing problems except themselves. So I found your column a great lead-in to our course work.''

She began her class by asking her students to identify their goals, and she promised to send their letters to me at the end of the quarter. Here's what some of her students reported.

''It was a dumb idea, a worthless experiment, and a total waste of time. Who is this Wilbers character, anyway?''

Just kidding. Here's what they really wrote.

■ ''In just 10 short weeks, I've made significant progress in my writing skills. Best of all, I've gained new confidence in myself.''

■ "The suggestion that has been most helpful is writing every day. If anyone had told me at the beginning of January that I would enjoy writing, I wouldn't have believed it."

■ "Reading out loud felt awkward at first, but I found it to be very helpful."

■ "I have replaced unnecessary expressions such as 'until such time as' and 'due to the fact that' with shorter expressions such as 'until' and 'because.'"

■ "I started with the easy ones, which were to buy a dictionary and to read a book for fun and pleasure."

■ "I'm learning how to support my arguments with specific and concrete examples and evidence. My first assignments were full of my ideas but didn't give any evidence to prove my point."

■ "When writing my first draft I used to keep going back to revise. Now I write without stopping."

■ "I made a list of word pairs that I confuse, such as accept/except, affect/effect, board/bored, capital/capitol, lesson/ lessen, principal/principle, and the list goes on. Then I made a list of the five words I misspell most frequently. My list was much more then five."

■ "Making several passes through a document when proofreading [is a goal that] was never met and that may never be met in my lifetime."

■ "For my last four weeks, I have been reading out loud while editing, supporting my arguments with specific examples, using transitional words, and deleting unnecessary words."

■ "The best resolution has been learning to use a computer. This has opened up a whole new language to me, a wonderful method of writing and printing. Just this afternoon, Mr. Widdel, my WP Essentials instructor, personally handed my final test to me with a mark of A-92. WOW! He docked me five points because I used the 'l' letter for '1' many times within the 10 pages. This is a very difficult usage for me to change after 47 years of typing."

Mr. Widdel, five points for the same mistake? Have a heart!

Making it Short and Sweet

One MBA Executive's Writing Style: A Critique

It isn't every day you get an invitation like this one. One of my readers, a president and CEO of a small company, sent me a couple of writing samples with this note:

"Enclosed are examples of letters written by one of my MBA executives. We argue over the quality and composition of his letters. He claims to be an excellent writer of business letters. Am I crazy, or is the content and structure really awful?"

How's that? An open invitation to critique the writing of a real-life MBA executive. Care to join me?

Let's take this letter as an example:

"Enclosed please find a revised copy of the Representative Agreement we discussed on the telephone last Friday. Besides addressing the specific points you brought up with reference to your name, this revised copy addresses the question you raised regarding commissions at termination, by incorporating an additional reference in the third paragraph of the termination section.

"I have also included several minor revisions, so as to hopefully eliminate any possible confusions regarding any of the points made in the document.

"Provided you are satisfied with this revision, I would appreciate if you would sign one of the copies and return same to my attention, keeping the other for your own records.

"If you should want to make any further modifications, please feel free to contact me at your convenience.

"I look forward to hearing from you in the near future."

Well, is it *awful*? I don't think so. I do think it is overwritten, and this makes it sound affected and stiff, even a bit stuffy. But not awful. To be truly awful, in my opinion, the letter would have to combine wordiness with basic errors in grammar and punctuation. Here, the writer demonstrates good command of the language. The problem, as I see it, has more to do with tone and voice than with basic writing skills.

Here's one example of how the letter might be rewritten using more natural language:

"In response to the concerns you expressed to me on the phone last Friday, I have revised the Representative Agreement. (See enclosed copy.)

"The changes address the specific points you brought up regarding your name. By incorporating an additional reference in the third paragraph of the termination section, the revised version also addresses your question concerning commissions at termination.

"In addition, I have made several minor revisions to eliminate possible confusion elsewhere in the document.

"If you are satisfied with these revisions, please sign one of the copies and return it to me. Keep the other for your own records.

"If you want to make any additional modifications, please call me [OR: please give me a call].

"I look forward to hearing from you soon."

As you can see, my revisions seek to communicate the writer's thought in language that is both more conversational and more concise. The specific changes are: "Enclosed please find a revised copy of the Representative Agreement" to "I have revised the Representative Agreement. (See enclosed copy.)"; "with reference to" to "regarding"; "the question you raised" to "your question"; "so as to hopefully eliminate any possible confusions regarding any of the points made in the document" to "to eliminate possible confusion elsewhere in the document"; "provided you are satisfied" to "if you are satisfied"; "I would appreciate if you would sign" to "please sign"; "return same" to "return it"; "if you should want" to "if you want"; "further modifications" to "additional modifications"; "please feel free to contact me at your convenience" to "please call me" or "please give me a call"; and "in the near future" to "soon."

The overall effect of these changes is to project an image of down-to-earth approachability rather than distant formality.

Remember: To be fully effective, business correspondence should reflect the style and character of American society. What most people want these days is writing that is not only precise and professional but also personal.

Send Your Boss to Language Efficiency School

I've seen some bad cases of wordiness before, but this one beats all.

It was written by O. Lee Mackerel, President and CEO of a small, tight-knit firm called Undies Unlimited, and sent to me by Francis Fuddydud, the firm's Vice President for Marketing, with this note: "Help! My boss has been writing things like this for years. Everyone who must read his writing suffers horribly. What can we do?"

I'll let the memo speak for itself:

"At this point in time, I am experiencing considerable difficulty in understanding how we can possibly proceed with the release of our new line of men's underwear for the reason that it appears wholly evident that a certain number of our employees are in total and complete disagreement in regard to the matter of anticipated customer demand.

"As a matter of fact, my personal belief in this matter is that I do not believe that there is necessarily any harm and/or inconsistency in waiting to introduce and/or initiate this exciting new product at this point in time until such time as our market analysis study has been completely finalized, which may take another month or so in time.

"Irregardless of my non-objection, however, and despite the fact that we all desire to keep things progressing forward in a positive direction, in the final analysis I cannot help but say that I deem the action of postponement absolutely and wholly advisable.

"Meanwhile, please let me know at your earliest convenience as to whether or not you think we should proceed with the difficult and potentially risky process of releasing this product. I certainly hope and trust that I will continue to have occasion to interface with all of you in positive ways on this matter in the foreseeable future and/or until such time as we can finally make a decision.''

Well, I must admit, that's painful. It's an evident and clear-cut case of unrelenting verbosity of a profusely grandiloquent, effusively loquacious nature. In a word, it's wordy. I count 50 instances of redundancies such as ''personal belief'' and ''completely finalized''; fancy language such as ''deem'' and ''to have occasion''; and wordy expressions such as ''for the reason that'' (in place of ''because'') and ''until such time'' (in place of ''until''). How many can *you* find?

The first phrase of the second paragraph reminds me of something Mark Twain once said: '''As a matter of fact' precedes many a statement that isn't.'' Regarding ''the foreseeable future,'' Strunk and White offer this comment in *The Elements of Style*: ''A cliché, and a fuzzy one. How much of the future is foreseeable? Ten minutes? Ten years? Any of it? By whom is it foreseeable? Seers? Experts? Everybody?''

And therein lies the problem. Wordy language is not only annoying but fuzzy, and fuzzy language begets fuzzy thought. The solution? Language Efficiency School.

That's right. Now you can send your word-smitten boss to Language Efficiency School. With a motto of ''LES is BES,'' Language Efficiency School offers a patented Verbosity Reduction Method, which features intensive tutoring and shock therapy along with periods of enforced silence.

How effective is the program?

Well, no educational institution can guarantee success, but if O. Lee Mackerel's experience is any indication, the results are truly astonishing. Here, for example, is how Mackerel revised his memo after only two months in residence at LES:

''I am postponing for one month the release of our new line of men's underwear. That should give our marketing division time to complete its study. Meanwhile, if you have any concerns about whether this product will sell, let me hear them.''

How's that? Compared with the original version, it's as refreshing as outdoor baseball in Minnesota.

Pseudo-sophistication No Justification for Obfuscation

William Hanvik of Minneapolis writes: "As a lifelong wordsmith and a graduate in journalism from the U of Minn., I've always deplored the roundabout, pseudo-sophisticated way some people talk and write, apparently in an effort to appear erudite.

"In rereading a memo that was sent to me a few years ago, I still don't know what the author was trying to say—do you? I *think* he meant, 'This is a tough job, but we're doing the best we can.'"

Here's the memo. What do *you* think?

"The determination of an effective, meaningful measure of the product development people/cost ratio proved to be a difficult challenge.

"Being a service department charged with a variety of tasks and responsibilities added to the complexity of the assignment.

"There are a number of factors which, when performed effectively, produce the desired results. These include the successful products introduction, meeting commitments on time, effective utilization of manpower and resources, and the maintenance of our existing line and its profitability.

"Our energies, applied to these factors, will improve the people/cost ratio in product development and affirmatively effect the ratios of all the departments we interface with.

"Measurement of the job, effectively completed, is at best only subjective. Our awareness of the goals and responsibilities coupled with the knowledge of the costliness of efforts applied in the wrong directions has to be the means by which we proceed. The successful completion of our responsibilities and attainment of our goals thus should be the measure of an improved people/cost ratio for product development."

Well, I must agree. Getting the meaning from that memo is tough sailing.

What makes people write in such a "roundabout, pseudo-sophisticated" style?

I suspect that the author may have felt defensive about his department's performance and therefore uncomfortable with his message. The result: an unconscious tendency to avoid direct statement.

Here are some specific traits of this indirect style:

■**Long subjects and delayed verbs**. Note the location of the main verbs, particularly in the memo's first two and last two sentences. Delaying the verbs postpones the message. The unnecessary comma in the last sentence is a giveaway. It suggests that the author, having created a long-winded subject, is apologizing for having kept the reader on hold.

■**Overuse of nominalizations**. Nominalizations are the noun forms of verbs and adjectives, as in "determination" for "determine," "introduction" for "introduce," and "completion" for "complete." Although nominalizations can be useful, here they are used excessively.

■**Wordiness**. Some indirection may be warranted in sensitive writing situations, but the author goes on too long. If the message is "our recommendations will be delayed," why not say so clearly?

Other problems include faulty parallelism in the sentence beginning "These include . . . ," misuse of "effect" for "affect" in the fourth paragraph, and a distracting mannerism of interruptions or asides ("when performed effectively," "applied to these factors," and "effectively completed").

Correcting these problems produces a memo that is not only clearer but nearly 100 words shorter:

"Improving the people/cost ratio for product development is a challenge.

"We are a service department charged with a variety of tasks and responsibilities. We must successfully introduce products, meet commitments on time, utilize manpower and resources effectively, and maintain our existing line and its profitability. These demands have delayed our progress.

"Nevertheless, we believe we can succeed in improving the people/cost ratio. You will receive our recommendations by the end of the month."

That's my response, but I like Hanvik's better:

"Sesquipedalian verbiage, efficaciously collated and paginated, conveys a heterogenous significance proportionate to the educational and cultural attainments of the fortuitous recipient. Pedagogical proliferations, ergo, employing a polysyllabic superfluity of morphemes, are to be eschewed with an earnest assiduity similar to that exhibited by the prudent mariner in shunning the hazardous concealed shoal. The intelligibility of a missive can well be obfuscated in such a manner as to become as unintelligible as a hieroglyphic to a Hottentot.

"In short, memos should be readable."

Bravo!

From Prewriting to Postwriting

The Five Elements of Effective Writing

Your reputation is on the line. After years of hard work, you have been promoted to the position of your dreams. Now it's time to deliver.

Your first assignment is to write a statement articulating your vision and goals. Your statement will be published in the company newsletter, where everyone, including your new boss, will read it. Although you have a reputation for being an excellent communicator, you're not sure you deserve it. Truth is, you have more confidence in your ability as a speaker than in your competence as a writer.

It doesn't help that you new boss, nicknamed "Chewy" (short for "Chew-'em-up-and-spit-'em-out"), has high expectations of you.

Here's what to do.

First, relax. Well, try to relax.

Next, tell your secretary you don't want to be interrupted, close your office door, water your plants, sit down, and write for five minutes without stopping to read or revise what you have written. Start with "What I really want to accomplish in my new position is . . . ," and go from there. Don't work hard. Just write. Remember, no stopping or revising.

Next, make an outline of your major points, call a trusted friend and ask for some suggestions, go out and talk with some people on your staff to see if they have any ideas, come back to your office, water your plants, and write your first draft. Don't hesitate to modify your outline as you go, and don't fuss over your introduction. You can fix that later.

Now, go home and relax. Talk with your significant other, play with your kids, walk the dog, read a book, watch some T.V., or go to a ball game. Try not to think about your article, especially when you are in bed falling asleep, but it's OK to dream about it.

In the morning, get to your office early, don't talk with anyone, close your door, water your plants, and write your second draft. Fax a copy to your trusted friend, then try to put it out of your mind while you wait for a response. If possible, allow a few days to pass without reading your draft. Once it has gone cold, read it again, keeping in mind any helpful suggestions from your friend. Depending on whom you know and trust in your new division, you might want to show it to a few people there.

Now you're ready for your final check. Use this checklist, which is organized according to the five elements of effective writing:

▪**CENTRAL IDEA**. Have you stated your purpose clearly and early? Is your material organized around a clear, manageable idea, argument, or thesis? Do your subordinate ideas support and reinforce your central idea?

▪**ORGANIZATION**. Have you arranged your material in a coherent and logical order? Have you kept the reader oriented to your central idea? Have you guided the reader between the divisions of your document with clear and helpful transitions? Does your conclusion summarize your argument, reiterate your central idea, suggest steps for implementation, and leave your reader with a sense of completion?

▪**SUPPORTING MATERIAL**. Have you offered sufficient explanations, examples, statistics, and quotations to support your ideas and make them meaningful and memorable to your reader? Are your examples specific, concrete, detailed, relevant, and persuasive? Are your quotations clearly related to your context and to your message?

▪**EXPRESSION**. Have you chosen language that is clear, accurate, and appropriate to the your purpose, audience, and material? Is your word choice unassuming, specific, and free of clichés and meaningless jargon? Are your sentences free of wordiness, ambiguity, and unnecessarily involved constructions?

▪**SPELLING, GRAMMAR, AND PUNCTUATION**. Have you eliminated errors in spelling, subject/verb agreement, noun/pronoun agreement, pronoun case, and parallel construction? Have you misplaced or omitted any commas or apostrophes?

You're finished. Now you've got nothing to worry about—except maybe your new associates, your staff, your budget, your job security, Chewy, and life in general.

To Overcome Writer's Block, Silence Inner Critic

Overcoming writer's block is easy. Just tell yourself to relax, think positive thoughts about your writing ability, and remind yourself that your first draft need not be perfect.

But if it's as easy as that, why have I been sitting here staring at this screen for two hours?

In exasperation, I call a friend, who says, "Your problem is obvious: You're unclear about your purpose in writing, you're intimidated by your audience, you're unsure you know what you're talking about, you're trying to write perfect copy in your first draft, and you're preoccupied with your weaknesses rather than your strengths as a writer."

"Oh. Thanks."

"Don't mention it," she says.

"Say, is there anything I can do to silence that negative voice?"

"Sure. Hang up."

"What?"

"Hang up whenever you hear it."

So I do, but that doesn't help. In a moment the phone rings.

"How's it going now?" she asks.

"I'm still stuck."

"No problem. Close your eyes. Imagine the year is 1976. It's spring. You're in upper state New York attending the Lake Saranac Writers Conference. One of the writers you meet is novelist Gail Godwin. She is sitting before a great stone hearth in a rustic lodge. Do you remember her advice about overcoming writer's block?"

"Yes."

"Start there." She hangs up.

Let's see. The room smells faintly of wood smoke. From every wall, stuffed animal heads gaze down on us in stern and dignified silence. The trick, Gail says, is to imagine that your inner, self-censoring voice is a little creature, what Freud called the "Watcher at the Gate," who sits perched on the edge of your subconscious mind. Even as your thoughts are first taking shape, this creature says things like, "Stupid. Unoriginal. Doesn't sound right. Don't let it out."

When this voice interferes with writing a first draft, look the Watcher at the Gate right in the eye and say, "Be quiet. I know you're there. You have a legitimate role to play, but you're too early. First I create. Then I revise."

The phone rings.

"That stinks."

I hang up. The phone rings again.

"Good. Now you're getting the idea. Don't listen to that other voice."

She hangs up.

Once you have silenced your inner critic, the words should just flow. But sometimes, inexplicably, they don't. Like now.

The phone rings.

"Now what's the matter?"

"I don't know. I'm still blocked. It's not that I'm being critical. My mind is wandering. I keep thinking about sailing. I have this little turbo catamaran, a racing boat with a jib and trapeze and a beautiful blue and purple sail that pops in the breeze when you bring it about. In a good wind, the mast hums and vibrates like a bumblebee."

"Stop. You're not concentrating. Get up from your desk and sit somewhere else. If you're using a word processor, try writing by hand. If you're writing by hand, try typing or using a dictaphone. Stand up and say out loud what you plan to write. Don't worry about how it sounds. Just say it. Write for five minutes without stopping to revise or read what you have written. Make a list of your major points. Write the easy parts first. Write the opposite of what you mean. Write about something else, anything, even sailing. Now, get started."

"What if none of that works?" I ask.

"Read Peter Elbow's *Writing without Teachers* or Natalie Goldberg's *Writing Down the Bones*. They understand the psychology of writing as well as anyone."

She hangs up.

I think I'll take her advice. After all, I could read Elbow and Goldberg on my sailboat.

Reinstate the Quality Loop
To Ensure Good Writing

In 1964 John Fielden wrote one of the most influential and most frequently reprinted articles ever published by the *Harvard Business Review*, ''What do you mean I can't write?''

In that article, he sought to help managers move beyond telling their employees, ''You simply can't write,'' to explaining to them ''in specific, meaningful terms'' exactly what was wrong with their writing. To accomplish this, he concentrated on four elements of effective business writing, each of which he broke into subcategories and examined in checklist fashion.

Fielden postulated that one might attain:

■**Readability** by attending to the reader's level, sentence construction, paragraph construction, familiarity of words, reader direction, and focus;

■**Correctness** by attending to mechanics, format, and coherence;

■**Appropriateness** by attending (in upward communications) to tact, supporting detail, opinion, and attitude, and (in downward communications) to diplomacy, clarification of desires, and motivational aspects;

■**Thought** by attending to preparation, competence, fidelity to assignment, analysis, and persuasiveness.

Much of his advice seems as relevant and cogent today as it did the day his article was published, but one paragraph stands out.

To support his point that grammar and punctuation mistakes ''are hardly the most important aspects of business writing,'' Fielden wrote: ''The majority of executives are reasonably well educated and can, with a minimum of effort, make themselves adequately proficient in the 'mechanics' of writing. Furthermore, as a man rises in his company, his typing (at least) will be done by a secretary, who can (and should) take the blame if a report is poorly punctuated and incorrect in grammar, not to mention being presented in an improper 'format.'''

My, how times have changed.

First, it no longer seems certain that the majority of executives can achieve proficiency in the ''mechanics'' of writing ''with a minimum of effort.'' Second, we now think in terms of both men *and* women rising in their companies, and we take care to use language that reflects this awareness. And third, for many executives the personal secretary has been replaced by the word processor, and the person who operates the word processor is—you know who.

The last change has both empowered and impoverished many of us. Personal computers have placed at our fingertips an immense wealth of information. They have greatly simplified the process of creating, manipulating, storing, and reusing text. And they have given us the awesome ability to send our text to nearly anyone, nearly anywhere, at the push of a button.

This means that many executives who formerly depended on others to help them get their message across must now depend on their own skills as writers, editors, and proofreaders—with nothing more than a clever machine backing them up. No longer do they routinely hand their rough drafts or hastily dictated tapes to a competent secretary who can be trusted to ''make it right'' (and who can be blamed if something is wrong).

The result for some companies has been disastrous. The overall quality of writing has plummeted. Too often customers have been shocked, even angered, by the shoddiness of the communications they receive from what they had previously considered a reputable firm staffed by competent and conscientious professionals. One even hears of word-processed reports sent to high-paying clients with the wrong name appearing somewhere in the document.

With all the emphasis today on Total Quality Management, isn't it time we did more to ensure quality control of something that is so closely linked to our image and reputation?

I recommend two possible solutions:

■Reinstate the office editor, the "expert" who can be trusted to catch 90 percent of the problems that might embarrass you or your company.

■Pair every writer with an editing partner who can be counted on to catch at least the most egregious errors.

Either way, make this your standard operating procedure: Let nothing leave the office that has been seen by only one pair of eyes.

Between You and Me

Wanted: Top-level Managers
To Edit Staff Writing

Have I got the job for you: Copy editing!

Now, you may be thinking you have more important duties in your portfolio—responsibilities such as overseeing the department budget, developing the leadership skills of your managers, or shaping your company's strategic planning. These are nothing, however, compared to the importance of copy editing. Truly effective managers find time to revise every document written by every subordinate in their division.

In case you have failed to become a full-time copy editor, here's how to get the job.

■**Don't trust anyone**. No one can hold the line on good, quality writing as well as you can. Resist the temptation to delegate. Read everything. How else can you catch the errors?

■**Create a threatening atmosphere**. Nothing makes people write better than fear. State your standards in no uncertain terms. Use ridicule as a motivator. A good technique is to talk disparagingly about people's writing skills behind their backs. Try to make even your most competent writers feel inadequate. Otherwise, they start getting ideas.

■**Avoid giving clear and coherent instructions**. As a general rule, say as little as possible about an assignment. Why burden people with details? The worst mistake you can make is to give them something in writing.

■**Cultivate an eccentric style of communication**. You might want to emulate one of the three styles described by Barbara Von Diether in "Righting Rotten Writing" (*Training* magazine, April 1992). Method 1 is to race by on your way out the door, throw stuff on your writer's desk, and say, "Take care of this, will you?" Method 2, called "progressive revelation," involves revealing more and more information about what you want the closer it gets to the deadline. Every time your writer talks to you or sends you a draft, reveal some new piece of information. Method 3 is communicating "by little words on yellow sticky notes" and then adding a bunch of stuff you never mentioned when it comes time to revise. With practice, you can make any of these styles work for you.

■**Once you've made your assignment, pretend it doesn't exist**. Act as though you are too preoccupied with other matters to answer questions. Body language can be especially effective in communicating your general unapprochability. If you show any interest in how things are going, you risk suggesting that writing is a process that may be discussed at any of its various stages. Can you imagine where this might lead? Whatever you do, don't request a working draft.

■**Avoid being specific about deadlines**. Because they only distract your writers, deadlines are better left unmentioned. The next best thing is to give an unreasonable deadline. Another option is to give what appears to be a reasonable deadline and then move it forward without warning.

■**Interrupt the writing process as often as possible**. Interruptions destroy a writer's concentration. Carefully timed, they can delay completion of a writing project by hours and, with persistence on your part, by days.

■**Always change something**. Never let a document cross your desk without changing *something*, even if it's just a comma. As a matter of principle, every document, even one that appears to be flawless, should be revised. Over time, even your most tenacious writers will begin to lose heart. You'll know you're making progress when the quality of the copy people give you begins to deteriorate.

■**Never explain *why* you have changed something**. My motto is "Keep 'em guessing." If you reveal your rules of writing and your principles of style, people may start following them on their own. This will leave you feeling unneeded and lonely.

■**Write poorly yourself**. Here's the real kicker. Now that you've got them smarting over the way you rewrite *their* writing, show them some of *your* writing that is studded with grammatical errors and weighted down with convoluted, tortured sentences.

Remember: Your most important duty as a manager is copy editing. After all, if you weren't spending all your time revising and rewriting other people's writing, what else would you be doing?

Trust Is Key to Cross-racial Writing Criticism

Our language is close to our hearts. Our choice of words reflects our identity and our intelligence. And when our words, particularly our written words, are criticized or called into question, we feel attacked.

Nowhere is this more true than in criticism given across racial lines.

Consider, for example, the dynamics of a white supervisor reviewing a report written by a black employee. How does this interaction differ from an exchange involving two people of the same race? What can both parties do to overcome the racial tension that can accompany these encounters? What can both parties do to ensure a successful outcome?

Here are some practical tips on how to offer and receive cross-racial criticism, whether the interaction is between a white supervisor and a black employee, a black supervisor and a white employee, or any combination of races working together in positions of unequal power.

SUPERVISOR/CRITIC

■**Approach editing as a collaborative process built on trust and respect.** Your purpose as critic is to help the writer create the most effective document possible, not to put the writer down.

■**Invite questions.** It is sometimes difficult for people of different races to talk openly and candidly, especially when one person is below the other in the organizational hierarchy, so make it easy for your writer to ask for clarification.

■**Begin your critique on a positive note.** Recognize the writer's strengths before pointing out the writer's weaknesses.

■**Don't overwhelm the writer with too many suggestions at once.** If you are generally dissatisfied with the writer's performance or skill level, try editing in stages, identifying and working on a few key points at a time.

■**Make the editing process educational for the writer.** Don't just hand back corrected copy. Look for patterns of errors, identify the errors by category, correct the first few occurrences, then ask the writer to correct the rest.

■**Allow the writer as much flexibility in style and approach as possible.** There is often more than one right way to write something. When you do make changes, explain your revisions carefully and respectfully—in person, if appropriate.

SUBORDINATE/WRITER

■**Don't expect perfection of yourself or your writing.** Even the most effective writers make mistakes.

■**Accept constructive criticism as a normal part of the writing process.** Its purpose is to improve content, expression, and style.

■**Try not to take criticism personally.** Even the most successful writers produce imperfect copy. Nearly everyone, no matter how accomplished, can benefit from the suggestions of a good editor.

■**Invite criticism.** Make it easy for your supervisor to make suggestions. Not only does your taking the initiative demonstrate confidence and professionalism, but it opens the door for coaching on how to improve your performance. Remember: What you don't hear may hurt you more than what you do.

■**Assume that your critic has your best interests in mind, unless you have reason to believe otherwise.** If you don't understand why a revision is being suggested, ask for an explanation.

■**Challenge criticism that you believe is racially motivated or that you feel reflects racial insensitivity.** Whether you use direct confrontation or quiet diplomacy depends on your style and situation, but you have a right to fair and unbiased treatment.

I don't pretend to understand all the complexities of America's complicated race relations. I suspect that few people do. But I do believe that the key to successful cross-racial criticism is trust. If both critic and writer understand and feel comfortable with their roles, the sometimes delicate process of creating and editing text can bring both parties together rather than drive them apart.

Successful Dictation Depends on Collaboration

I love being a writing consultant.

It has deepened my knowledge of language, broadened my understanding of the world of commerce, and increased my appreciation for the varied settings and cultures in which on-the-job writing takes place. They say we English majors don't get out much, but being a writing consultant gives me a chance to snoop on people's professional lives.

One of my more exciting assignments is getting called in to negotiate an office dispute. Sometimes the issue is as basic as the location of the comma: Does it go inside or outside the quotation marks? (It goes inside.) Other times the conflict has deteriorated to the point of all-out warfare. Usually the clash is between the people who generate text and those who prepare it.

The other day, for example, I got an emergency call from a desperate client, who shouted into the receiver: "Steve, come quick! It's getting ugly!" Without pausing to don protective clothing, I leapt into my CommaMobile and sped across town. The scene I encountered was indeed nasty.

On one side of the room were the middle- and upper-level managers who dictated all their correspondence and reports. On the other side were the secretaries and word processing staff whose job it was to make sense of the unintelligible grunts and wheezes that came through their headphones by the hour. Tempers had reached a fever pitch.

"If you don't know how to spell someone's name, why don't you just ask me?" shouted one manager, who ducked as a bottle of white-out correction fluid hurled past and splatted on the wall behind.

"Why don't you delete the paragraphs you don't want included instead of telling me to skip them after I've already typed them?'' yelled one secretary, who took a blow to the shoulder with a pocket-sized dictionary. ''Haven't you ever heard of a rewind button?''

Both sides were reaching for the heavy office equipment when I intervened. At the sound of my voice, there was instant calm. It usually works that way.

''OK, here's what the people who generate text should do,'' I said.

■**Speak in your normal voice and enunciate clearly**. If you need to pause, turn off the machine or simply stop speaking rather than use fillers such as ''uh'' or ''er.''

■**Spell out names the first time you use them**. Even common names have more than one spelling (such as Andersen and Anderson).

■**Indicate punctuation**. Take special care to specify new paragraphs and paired punctuation marks such as quotation marks and parentheses.

■**Use the rewind feature to correct a word or phrase**. This saves time and frustration for the text preparer.

■**Clearly indicate when you have reached the end of a document**. This too saves time and confusion.

■**Expect accuracy, but take responsibility for final proofreading**. Certain errors can be detected only by the author.

Next I said, ''Now here's what the text transcribers should do.'' By this time the warring factions had returned to their desks and were quietly taking notes.

■**Use standard spelling**. If you are unsure what word is intended, mark your question on the copy.

■**Take responsibility for correcting obvious errors in punctuation, grammar, and usage**. Find out how much latitude your boss will allow you. Keep at your desk a good reference guide (such as *The Gregg Reference Manual*) and use it.

Finally, I offered this last bit of advice: ''Successful collaboration in writing depends on two common elements: common sense and common courtesy.''

As I turned to go, everyone was smiling. Last I heard, the two sides were planning a winter retreat to the Bahamas. I do love this work.

Connecting through Correspondence

Sales Letters Succeed by Linking Product to Need

A simple formula for writing a successful sales letter has three parts: Know your product, know your customer, and link the two.

Here's how you can make this formula work for you the next time you write a sales letter.

First, take the time to know your product or service. What makes it valuable? What makes it unique? How does it compare to other products on the market?

Next, ask the same type of questions about your prospective customers. Who are the people most likely to need or want your product? What are their values and prejudices? How can you appeal to their beliefs and feelings?

Now that the hard work is over, you're ready to do the easy part: Write a letter that links your product's benefits to your customer's needs.

Here's my advice on how to accomplish that.

Sales letters, like most things in life, have a beginning, a middle, and an end. These are commonly called the opening, the body, and the closing. Each component, in turn, has three basic functions.

■**OPENING**

■Catch your reader's attention.

■Connect with your reader by using the "you viewpoint" (or writing from the reader's perspective).

■Arouse interest in your product or service.

■**BODY**

■Focus on your most powerful selling point.

■Describe your product in terms of its benefits to your reader.

■Provide evidence supporting the value of your product.

■CLOSING

■Tell how to purchase your product or obtain your service (by returning an enclosed card, calling, faxing, etc.).

■Offer an incentive for your reader to take immediate action.

■Emphasize how easy it is for your reader to respond (and make sure it *is* easy).

Let's take a poorly written opening as an example:

"Please find enclosed a brochure that lists our lawn care services. Our highly recommended weekly treatment plan can be obtained at the low cost of $65 per treatment, which we ask that you pay in advance."

Here's how that opening might be revised to catch the reader's attention, to connect with the reader by using the "you viewpoint," and to arouse interest in the product:

"Tired of digging, spraying, and fighting weeds that can make your lawn look like a playground for pachyderms? If you would rather spend your weekends relaxing at the lake or having fun on the golf course, leave the hassle of lawn care to us. The enclosed brochure will tell you how our total-service plan can give you a beautiful, trouble-free lawn all summer long."

Now that you know the three-part formula, you can use this checklist to ensure that your letter will produce results.

☐Message is presented clearly and succinctly.

☐Product is described in terms of how it will benefit reader.

☐"You viewpoint" is sustained throughout.

☐Language is friendly and engaging.

☐Tone is personal.

☐Paragraphs are short, well organized, and sharply focused (with particular care given to the opening).

☐Text is highlighted using standard techniques (bold, under-lined, and italicized type, bulleted or numbered items presented in a column, etc.; for a more personal look, paragraphs are in-dented and right margins are ragged, or unjustified).

☐Presentation and format are professional in appearance (copy is free of distracting errors in grammar, spelling, and punctuation).

□"Stoppers" have been eliminated (as defined by professional fund-raisers, a "stopper" is anything that causes the reader to stop reading, from a poorly worded sentence to a sexist word or phrase).

□P.S. persuasively restates main selling point or emphasizes how easy it is to take the desired action (in persuasive writing, the P.S. is more than an afterthought; it's your last opportunity to make an impression).

As a final check, test your copy on prospective buyers. After all, why leave something as important as sales to guesswork, even if you *are* acting on good advice?

Openings Are Key to Successful Sales Letters

If there's one thing your prospective customers probably don't have, it's time—time for you, time for your advertising, even time for themselves.

Knowing this is key to writing an effective sales letter. These days it seems as though you have only nanoseconds to grab your readers' attention. If your opening doesn't do its job, your letter goes unread.

The number one rule to getting your letter off to an effective start is to write from your readers' perspective. To do this, begin not by describing your product or service but by appealing to your readers' interests, needs, or desires. Only after you have caught the attention of your readers should you begin trying to convince them that what you have is what they want.

Here are some examples of attention-getting openings that might help you connect with potential customers:

■**Offer of dramatic savings** "We can provide you more dependable courier service at half the price you now are paying."

■**Offer of a gift, free trial, or coupon** "As a busy office supervisor who has only limited time for shopping—and no time for mistakes in purchasing—you will be pleased to know that you can shop for all your office needs through OfficeNet, a new, interactive computer network now available in your area. Call today for free installation and a no-obligation, 30-day trial."

■**Appeal to customer's need or desire** "Are you tired of getting sales calls at the dinner hour but afraid that if you don't answer you'll miss an important call from a friend? Now there's a device that screens those calls and automatically plays back an appropriate pre-recorded response."

■**Thought-provoking question or surprising statistic** "When was the last time you checked to see how much your company was spending on duplicating? You may be paying two to three times more than your competition pays for the same volume of copying."

■**A clever or engaging quotation** "Andrew Jackson once said, 'I have no respect for a man who knows only one way to spell a word.' Well, the planners at Creative Retreats Conference Center have no respect for any team of consultants who know only one way to help you boost your employees' morale and productivity."

■**A touching or dramatic anecdote** "In 1984 Jane Williams survived a 2,000-foot fall when her parachute failed to open. She landed in three feet of water in a farmer's pond and waded to shore without a scratch. Now she volunteers her time as a nurse's aid helping veterans who weren't so lucky."

■**A testimonial or celebrity endorsement** "'I was so impressed with Mill City Flour's success in entering the fiercely competitive cereal market,' said marketing expert Thomas Quin, 'that I decided to investigate.' Here's what he found about how we do business."

■**An apology linked to a sales proposal** "Your disappointment with how long it took us to deliver your last order is of great concern to us here at the Muffin Shop, where we pride ourselves on quick, dependable service. I apologize for the inconvenience and embarrassment our delay caused you. To make it up to you, I am offering you a special 20 percent discount on your next order."

Remember: To determine if you have written a successful opening to your sales letter, check to see if you have used the "you viewpoint." Then ask yourself two questions (in this order): Will this catch my readers' attention? Will this arouse interest in my product or service?

As always, the surest way to know is to test your copy on a sampling of prospective buyers.

DOs and DON'Ts for Writing Holiday Greetings

Well, it's that time of year again. Time to get in the holiday spirit, time to count our blessings, time to hope for a better world, and time to spend more money than we can afford.

It's also a good time to re-establish ties with friends and acquaintances. Goodwill letters to customers, colleagues, and employees are an important part of the season.

Here are some **DOs** and **DON'Ts** for sending your holiday greetings.

DOs

■Mail early to avoid the rush and to make certain that your greeting arrives on time.

■Offer a greeting that creates goodwill.

■Express appreciation for your friendship or business relationship.

■Use commercially printed greeting cards, form letters, handwritten letters, or individually word-processed letters, depending on the expectations of your readers.

■Consider sending letters rather than cards because letters can be written in a more personal style and can contain more information.

■Combine a sales letter with a seasonal message, if appropriate.

DON'Ts

■Assume that everyone is celebrating the same religious holiday.

■Express religious sentiments, unless you know your readers well and you know they share your beliefs.

■Send a commercially printed greeting card or form letter without a handwritten note.

■Use titles when having your name printed on a card (for example, not "Dr. Stephen Wilbers" or "Mr. Stephen Wilbers" but "Stephen Wilbers" or "Steve Wilbers").

■Send an overly aggressive sales message that may be perceived as self-serving and materialistic. As Rosalie Maggio points out in *How To Say It*, "Although no other period of the year is more commercial than the Christmas season, people don't like to be reminded of it."

Here's an example of a holiday greeting you might send to your customers. I wrote it myself:

> *Another year has come and gone;*
> *I wish I felt more blessed.*
> *I never really planned on*
> *Becoming this depressed.*
>
> *If you, like me, feel crummy,*
> *If you, like me, feel blue,*
> *Why don't you spend some money?*
> *I have to eat, like you.*

I worked hard on that, so I hope you like it. You may find, however, that my attempt at greeting card verse is a tad too direct for some of your customers. Here's an example of a goodwill/business greeting expressed with more subtlety:

"During this season of hope and gratitude, I wanted to let you know how much we at Galvanized Steel Products appreciate your loyalty as a customer.

"For 10 years now you have demonstrated your commitment to the highest standards in the industry by purchasing our fine quality steel products. We value your business—and we look forward to continuing to serve you for many years to come.

"Please accept our warmest wishes for a joyous and wonderful holiday season."

Now, I don't want you to think I'm cheap, but it occurs to me that this column might serve as a convenient holiday greeting to my own clients. So if any of you are reading this, I wish you all the best.

Think of the postage I'll save.

How To Say, "You're Wrong," Yet Keep Business

Telling someone he or she is wrong isn't easy—especially if the person you're telling is an important client. It's hard to find the right words. It's hard to convey your message in a tone that is firm but diplomatic. It's hard to disagree without offending. If you blow it, you risk losing your client's business.

Often it's easier just to let it go.

There comes a time, however, when the issue is too important or the principle too fundamental to compromise. That's when you could use some advice about how to write a customer relations letter that says, in essence, "I don't agree with you, but I still want your business."

Here's a five-part formula that might help:

■**Goodwill Greeting:** Open your letter on a positive note and in a personal tone. State your purpose for writing clearly but diplomatically.

■**Acknowledgement of reader's perspective:** Recognize your reader's point of view. Use language that shows empathy or understanding for that perspective without compromising your own position.

■**Statement of your position:** State your argument clearly and concisely. Stick with the main issue. Don't go on too long.

■**Action statement:** If some action is necessary to resolve the issue, be clear and specific about what that action is. Use language that is neutral and non-confrontational.

■**Goodwill closing:** Remind the reader of your respect and goodwill. Stress the importance of your continuing relationship. There are many ways of wording this, but your basic message should be: "You matter to me."

Let's take a real-life example. A Twin Cities environmental services firm was asked to sign on as a subcontractor for a major project. The contractor insisted that payment be contingent on whether the contractor was paid. The president of the environmental firm objected to the provision but didn't want to lose the contract.

Here's the text of the letter she wrote, with some minor revisions on my part:

"Thank you for your letter of December 15. I agree; it is well past time that we conclude our negotiations and reach an agreement on this contract.

"Your desire to minimize your risk is understandable. Making your payment to us contingent on whether you yourself are paid is one way of reducing risk.

"I am surprised, however, that you consider this arrangement a 'common industry practice.' Our experience is quite different. Although on occasion clients will suggest this arrangement, we have always been successful in persuading them to reconsider. Furthermore, we do not require this of our own subcontractors. When they provide a service we have requested, we pay them whether or not we ourselves are paid. We may ask them to wait 60-90 days, but we always pay for work we order.

"Because you are an important customer, we don't want to jeopardize our relationship with you. If we must accept the provision that we will be paid only if you are paid, we will reluctantly do so. Please furnish me with a copy of your subcontract agreement reflecting this provision. I will sign it and return it to you immediately.

"Thank you for your patience and understanding in concluding this contract. And thank you for your business. We do appreciate it."

Well, that's the way the letter should be written. But composing a letter according to this formula is hard work. It involves painstaking strategy, skillful diplomacy, and delicate tact, to say nothing of several rewrites. In short, it's not much fun.

Now here's the letter you wish you could write:

"You can't be serious. We don't get paid unless you get paid? Why don't we just lend you $100,000 without asking you to repay us unless you make a profit? Try again."

The Electronic Revolution

How Word Processors Help and Hurt Our Writing

"People have been writing on paper, or papyrus, for four or five thousand years—long enough, anyway, to get into the habit," writes William Zinsser in *Writing with a Word Processor*. In other words, people knew what they were dealing with.

With the advent of computers, however, we find ourselves on new ground. These increasingly sophisticated electronic devices offer previously unimagined capabilities for producing, editing, and manipulating our text.

But do they really help us write more effectively? Is word-processed language necessarily better language?

Take for example that indispensable feature, the spell checker. Pre-PC, writers sometimes perpetuated certain misspellings, such as "accommodate" with a single "m," "questionnaire" with a single "n," and "occurrence" with a single "r" and an "-ance." It seemed the more frequently we saw these misspellings, the less likely we were to recognize them as incorrect. Spell checkers, by breaking the error loop, have all but eliminated many of these.

But spell checkers have their limitations, as so ably illustrated by Penny Harper's poem, "Spellbound" (originally posted on the Internet):

> *I have a spelling checker*
> *It came with my PC;*
> *It plainly marks four my revue*
> *Mistakes I cannot sea.*
> *I've run this poem threw it*
> *I'm sure your pleased too no.*
> *It's letter-perfect in it's weigh.*
> *My checker tolled me sew.*

Obviously, if you use the wrong word but spell it correctly, say "complement" for "compliment," the spell checker raises no objection.

Perhaps the most attractive feature of these electronic wizards is that mighty, pulsating cursor, which alights like an avenging Fury on an offending word or passage and enables the writer to make it vanish with the stroke of a key. What could be more gratifying? And if you change your mind, there's the restore function, which forgives you for being indecisive and retrieves your original text without requiring that you reenter it.

Word-processed text is language at a bargain. It comes cheap. It doesn't cost as much as it once did to create or modify. But what is the effect of this facile fluency? The computer may be wonderful for helping us whip off a first draft, but does it make us less committed to our words? Does it encourage wordiness? On the other hand, does ease in editing sometimes lead the writer (or perhaps the writer's boss) to tinker endlessly? When in this fluid process do we arrive at "final" copy?

In addition to ease in creating and manipulating text, software programs provide quick access to seemingly limitless amounts of information. If length is an issue, the computer will give us a word count in a flash. If we aren't satisfied with our word choice, we can punch up the thesaurus for lists of synonyms and antonyms. If we don't know what a word means, we can bring an entire dictionary to our screen. If we are having trouble organizing our thoughts, we can resort to an automatic outlining program. If we are unsure of our grammar or style, we can request the advice of a programmed editor. And if we are tried of writing variations of essentially the same message, we can create a template or boilerplate version that can be quickly adapted for multiple uses.

To question the usefulness of any of these wondrous capabilities is like declaring oneself opposed to early spring in Minnesota. Still, one wonders about the long-term effects. How is computer-assisted writing shaping our understanding, use, and appreciation of language? Is it altering the writer's fundamental relationship with text? Over time, will English be enriched or debased by the new technology?

Nobody knows for sure.

I suspect, however, that the future of English has more to do with how well we humans learn to command our language than with how well we make our machines serve as tools.

It's Writer vs. Machine in a Fight over Language

Announcer: In this corner we have author and syndicated columnist Hulk Wilbers. [*Yea!*] In this corner we have leading programmed grammar/usage/style checker Grammatik 5. [*Boo!*] Let's see if we can interview the two contestants before the fight begins. Hulk, what's your opinion of your opponent here?

Writer: Well, me and Grammatik 4 had a go-around a few years ago. I fed it this sentence, "I are a English teacher I don't use no bad grammar," and the only mistake it caught was the missing "n" of the article "a." I thought it was a piece of junk.

Announcer: You hear that, Grammatik?

Machine: Grammatik has 96 different grammatical attributes associated with words in its grammar dictionary. This extensive lexical database enables Grammatik to analyze words, phrases, clauses, sentences, and paragraphs. Proofreading with Grammatik is now far more accurate and reliable, including more sophisticated error detection and fewer false errors.

Announcer: There you have it, ladies and gentlemen. It's a grudge match, a fight over control of the English language. There's the bell! Hulk comes out swinging!

Writer: There is many problems facing you and i. One being a total and complete extreme lack of cooperation. Its obvious to anyone like you or myself, we need to talk turkey now, we ain't got no time to loose noway anyways, we doesn't want to flaunt the rules of grammer or flout our considerable knowledge.

Announcer: It's a low blow, folks. I count 18 errors.

Undaunted, Grammatik begins to whir and beep. Keep your eyes glued on that multi-colored screen!

Machine: Spelling capitalization error. Replace with ''I.'' The subject pronoun ''I'' should not be used in the object position. Replace with ''me.'' The plural subject ''problems'' requires a plural verb, not the singular verb ''is.'' Replace with ''are.'' This doesn't seem to be a complete sentence.

Announcer: Pretty impressive, folks, you gotta admit. And look here: If you don't know what an incomplete sentence is, just press this button for ''Writing Guide'' and up pops this succinct and clearly worded definition: ''To be complete, a sentence must have a subject (a noun or pronoun), a verb, and the ability to stand alone coherently,'' etc. The machine also gives examples, makes a cross reference to ''comma splice or fused sentence,'' and even provides relevant page references in standard writing guides such as Troyka's *Handbook for Writers*, Williams' *Style*, and Gordon's *The Transitive Vampire*. Wow!

Wait. There's more. The machine catches the ''its'' spelling error (yes!), the nonstandard verb form ''ain't,'' the double negative, and the unneeded ''s'' on ''anyways.'' It flags ''we doesn't'' for ''we don't,'' ''grammer'' for ''grammar,'' and the commonly confused ''flaunt'' and ''flout.''

Well, Hulk. Whatta you say now? Pretty slick, eh?

Writer: No way, man! The machine let the ludicrously redundant phrase ''total and complete extreme'' go without a buzz or murmur. It passed right over ''myself'' for ''me,'' saw nothing offensive about ''talk turkey,'' incorrectly identified ''we ain't got no'' as a passive construction, missed ''loose'' for ''lose,'' suggested ''Norway'' as a replacement for ''noway,'' and even after I corrected the confusing word pair, ''flaunt'' and ''flout,'' it kept flagging them.

Machine: Depending on how you count, Grammatik correctly identified 13 of 18 errors.

Writer: Yeah, but you lulled me into a false sense of security. Your flashy definitions led me to believe you would catch *all* basic errors. You ain't got no heart, man. You ain't got no taste. You ain't even got no ears.

Announcer: So, what's your assessment, Hulk?

Writer: My assessment? I gotta admit fighting this mechanized monster was fun. Maybe it'll make us writers spend a little more time revising our texts.

Announcer: Still think Grammatik is a piece of junk?

Writer: Naw, I wouldn't say that. I'd call it an *interesting* piece of junk. Hah!

Announcer: I don't know, folks. Sounds like sour grapes to me.

Writing with a Word Processor— A Personal History

University of Iowa's Computer Center, Iowa City, 1977. I have completed my Ph.D. course work and am now writing my dissertation. My topic is the history of the Iowa Writers' Workshop, the country's first graduate school for writers.

I am entering my text into the University's first word processor, which runs on a mainframe computer. My "terminal" has no monitor. In fact, it looks like a standard IBM Selectric typewriter. As I type, it produces a stack of punched computer cards. At the conclusion of my typing session, I will give this stack of cards to a technician, who will run them overnight.

The next morning I will pick up a copy of my text, which will be printed in numbered lines on oversized green paper. I will refer to those numbers when I make revisions. If I delete or add more than one line of text, however, the numbering will shift accordingly, and I'll have to count subsequent lines by hand to make additional changes. I won't be able to get a new printout with new numbers until the following morning. Still, the computer allows me to revise a 200-page document anywhere I like without having to retype the entire text. I recognize this capability as revolutionary.

My committee members have asked for many revisions in my draft. They expect the process of revising and retyping my copy to take me several weeks, perhaps months. Five days later Bill Murray, a novelist, will ask how I was able to produce a revised draft so quickly. When I describe the new technology, he will be intrigued but skeptical.

Johnston Hall, University of Minnesota, 1981. As Director of Student Academic Support Services, I am writing to 16,000 students and 600 faculty members in the College of Liberal Arts. I have already taken my document through several drafts. The last two I asked my secretary to type on letterhead, thinking that each was final copy but then finding one more thing I wanted to change.

Each revision required my secretary to retype the entire document. Now I want to change the wording in the first paragraph. There is nothing terribly wrong with the present wording, but the change would improve it slightly. My secretary, who has other pressing work to do, is losing patience. I send the letter as it is.

Basement Office, Minneapolis, 1993. As I move my fingers across the keyboard, these words appear on my screen as white letters against a blue background. When I'm not in the mood to write, turning on this machine helps me get started. When I get tired, interacting with this electronic companion helps me keep going. Its steady hum means business. I like seeing my text take shape as I compose.

To begin writing this column, I retrieve my list of 72 previously published columns and look over the titles. Next I skim through a second file where I have listed ideas for future columns. Then I browse through my ''scrap'' file to see if anything there grabs me. If I were writing a proposal to a prospective client, I would pull up a template and make some minor alterations rather than start from scratch.

I do some revising as I go. From time to time I check my thesaurus. Sometimes I'll change the wording just to see how it looks, only to change it back to the original. I use the spell checker not only to catch typos but to get a word count. (My limit is 650 words.)

When my draft is completed, I'll print it and set it aside for a couple days. Then I'll take it out, make changes on the paper copy, enter those changes on the computer, and then send both paper and disk copy to my editor.

The computer makes it so easy to move words around that sometimes I forget how hard it is to write.

Use the Computer To Help You Think and Write

In some ways, writers and computers were made for each other.

Even for people who love to write (I count myself among them), writing is sometimes tedious, frustrating work. It can be downright wearisome. The computer's gift to writers is to eliminate some of that tedium and frustration.

Here's how to use the computer to make not only the process of writing more enjoyable but the product more successful.

■**Planning, composing, and formatting.** Clear writing involves clear thinking. But if you're like most of us, your thoughts don't present themselves in perfectly organized, logical sequence. They tumble out in haphazard, disjointed fashion. The computer can help bring order to the chaos.

Just as writers traditionally have gathered their thoughts by jotting and scribbling on paper, you can use keyboard and screen to capture your ideas as they occur to you. In fact, if you're a good typist (or should I say "keyboardist"?), you can transcribe your thoughts more rapidly than you can on paper, and this speed makes you better able to keep pace with your mind and follow a train of thought. (Don't worry if you miss one—another usually will arrive soon.)

The difference between scribbling and keyboarding is mobility. On paper, the mechanics of arranging rough notes into a clear outline and then expanding them into draft form can be laborious. On computer, manipulating text is a snap.

Not only can you use the components of your outline as headings to organize and develop your material, but you can begin composing at any point in your document (Peter Elbow calls this "growing" your message). You can modify your design and move blocks of text freely as your document takes shape. You can use automatic pagination, headers, and footers to format your document. You can even use an automatic outlining program to help you organize your material and clarify your thinking.

■**Editing, revising, and proofreading.** Moving your cursor through your text is like traveling by helicopter over rough terrain. You can go anywhere you like, instantly and effortlessly. Words, sentences, and entire paragraphs can be modified or eliminated with a few simple key strokes (or mouse strokes). If you change your mind, the computer reaches into its temporary memory and restores your deleted words (or droppings) without troubling you with retyping. What could be more satisfying?

In addition to instant modifications, the computer offers instant access to extraordinary amounts of information. The thesaurus enables you to expand your word choice with lists of synonyms and antonyms. An on-line dictionary (if your computer has sufficient memory) will give you definitions and derivations. The spell checker will catch most misspellings. And the grammar checker will catch some (but not all) basic errors in grammar and usage, as well as identify incidence of passive voice, calculate the average number of syllables per word, words per sentence, and sentences per paragraph, and offer mindless but interesting stylistic advice.

■**Storing and retrieving.** Word processing can eliminate the need to start from scratch. By storing key documents in well-organized directories (with similar documents given similar names), you can build on your best efforts. Your most persuasive proposal can serve as a model for your subsequent requests. Your most successful fund-raising letter can be modified for multiple uses. Your best thank-you letter can be adapted and embellished in moments. Even the simplest macro can save you time by bringing to your screen a standard format that includes your name and the current date.

Despite these benefits, the computer has its limitations. Although one part of writing involves moving words around—and if there's one thing the computer is good at it's moving things around—another, more fundamental part of writing involves knowing words and how to use them. Writers must still depend on the basic human qualities of knowledge and skill.

So use the computer to your advantage, but remember this: The secret of good writing is to learn how to write.

The Elements of Smile

Humor Can Establish Common Ground with Your Reader

It's time to get serious. After all, business writing is no laughing matter.

Or is it? Anyone who has been reading this column for the past year or so knows my answer.

To neglect humor as a means of communicating is, in my opinion, to neglect one of the most powerful tools we have for connecting with our readers. Used appropriately, humor can remind us of what we have in common as human beings. It can make us feel close when me might otherwise feel distant.

Consider, for example, a memo that begins, ''Although our annual budget review is tedious work, it's time to begin the process,'' with a memo that begins, ''Once again, it's that eagerly anticipated time of year: annual budget review.''

Which is better?

Well, that depends. The first opening is straightforward, dull, and safe; the second is intended to be lighthearted but risks sounding sarcastic. You be the judge.

Let's take another example. Your new boss is making her first presentation to her staff. At the beginning of her presentation, she drops her marker. As she stoops to pick it up, she says, ''Sorry. I washed my hands this morning and I can't do a thing with them.''

Does this make her appear foolish or good humored?

I would argue that, in most situations, people who can laugh at themselves not only reveal their human side but demonstrate self-confidence. If after cracking a joke at her own expense your boss then delivers a brilliant presentation, what would your impression be? Would her self-depreciating joke make you think less of her as a professional?

To help you decide when it is appropriate to risk using humor, let me offer three guidelines. Humor is clearly *inappropriate* when:

■Someone is asking you for a serious response.

■Your attempt at humor detracts from someone else's desire to communicate a serious point.

■Your intent is to insult or show malicious disrespect for an individual, group, or race (sexist jokes and racial slurs being the two most obvious examples).

Furthermore, certain types of humor seem to work better than others in professional settings. Here's a list of some common types, moving generally from the riskiest to the safest:

■**An involved narrative joke ending with a punch line**. Few of us can tell jokes well, and the time required to tell them may try the audience's patience. A poorly told joke is awkward for both teller and audience.

■**Puns or plays on words**. Some people love them; others hate them. The English, for example, consider a good pun a sign of intelligence; Americans tend to groan. Like Samuel Johnson, I find them punishing.

■**Irony, or using words to express something other than their literal meaning** (sometimes called "Socratic irony" because Socrates liked to play dumb when asking his students hard questions). Irony often involves saying the opposite of what you mean. This can add emphasis to a statement, as when you compliment someone by saying, "You're no dummy" or "I wish you would work harder." Of the two common types of irony, understatement or meiosis is generally better received than overstatement or hyperbole, as in "This assignment required more than a few minutes" as opposed to "This assignment took years."

■**Self-depreciating humor**. Making a joke at your own expense is one of the safest types of humor. Its only real risk is overdoing it to the point that you portray yourself as a buffoon.

■**Wit** (from the Old English *witan*, "to know"). John Locke defined this all-inclusive type of humor as, "The assemblage of ideas, and putting those together with quickness and variety.'' The effect is a comic twist or surprise, as when Peter De Vries said, ''I love being a writer. What I can't stand is the paperwork.''

Well, there you have my thoughts on humor. I recommend that you give it a try. But if you get yourself into hot water, don't blame me.

The War of the Words—
Invasion of the Bureaucrats

By Orson Welbers

A few years ago (it was 1938, as I recall) I did a little radio drama on the subject of business writing. In that broadcast I warned people of an impending disaster, a crisis in human discourse and communication. With infinite complacency, however, my compatriots went about their little affairs, serene in the assurance that, as long as they believed fervently in their message, the words would take care of themselves.

Now, I don't want anyone to panic, but the result has been catastrophic. American business writing as we once knew it has been destroyed. In its ashes has arisen an alien form of discourse: bureaucratese.

Excuse me. Something just came in on my fax. It's a bulletin from Worldwide NewsNet. Something about several explosions of incandescent gas occurring at regular intervals on the planet Mars. No cause for alarm, I'm sure.

The word "bureaucracy" has an intriguing history. It comes to us from the Old French "burel," the name of a woolen cloth used to cover desks, which became known as "bureaux." In time, the word "bureaux" was associated with the office, then with the occupants of the office. Add "-cracy" (from the Greek "kratos" meaning "power"), and you've got "bureaucracy."

Excuse me. Another bulletin just in. It seems that a huge flaming object, believed to be a meteorite, has fallen on a farm in the neighborhood of Grover's Mill, N. J., 22 miles from Trenton. Investigators are rushing to the scene.

Bureaucratese is writing characterized by general inscrutability, lifelessness, and lack of humanity. More specifically, its traits include:

■**Long and unnecessarily complex sentences**—examples abound.

■**Overuse of the passive voice**—sentences in which the subject is acted upon, as in "The report was written by me" or "A new method for effecting the dephosphorization of taconite pellets was developed by the University of Minnesota."

■**Excessive use of nominalizations**—nouns created from verbs, such as "contribution," "recommendation," and "consideration," as in "make a contribution," "offer a recommendation," and "take into consideration," rather than "contribute," "recommend," and "consider."

■**Long compound noun phrases**—series of nouns used as adjectives, such as "an acquisition candidate identification process" rather than "a process for identifying candidates for acquisition."

Wait a minute. There's something on the radio now. It's a live report from Grover's Mill in the Jersey farmlands. The meteorite has been located. Half-buried in a vast pit, it is curiously smooth, its surface unmarked by its passage through the earth's atmosphere. In fact, it doesn't look like a meteorite at all. It looks more like a huge cylinder made of yellowish-white metal.

Remember: Our goal as business writers is to connect with our readers, not to create distance through artificial-sounding language. At its best, business writing conveys a sense of our individuality, our humanity, and our warmth.

What's this? The cylinder appears to be hollow. A part of it is turning, as though its lid is unscrewing. Oh, no! Creatures are emerging. This can't be! The creatures. They're . . . they're . . . *bureaucrats*! An army of them!

It goes deeper than language. It goes to the heart of human interaction. To write with a sense of humanity is to recognize writing as a personal transaction between writer and reader. We must never forget that behind our words, behind this artifice of language, are real persons, authentic human beings.

The bureaucrats are armed with heat rays whose source of energy appears to be polished parabolic mirrors of unknown composition. Oh, no! They're pointing their weapons this way. In a flash of blinding heat my simple declarative sentences begin to convolute into grotesque structures, my verbs nominalize into lethargic globs, my thoughts solidify into rigid noun compounds.

I take refuge on the roof of my house. When I look down to the Minnehaha Creek, I see all manner of boats overloaded with fleeing population.

You and I may soon be the only humans left. Please. Write with humanity. Before it's too late!

New SlumberWrite Software "Revolutionizes" Writing

After 10 years of painstaking research, costly development, and meticulous testing, SlumberWrite, a revolutionary software program that promises to transform the world of business writing, is now available.

Created by Verb Those Nouns, Inc., SlumberWrite renders standard business prose into a soporific style so powerful that it is guaranteed to anesthetize even the most alert and conscientious reader. At the stroke of a key, it will automatically "slumberize" your text according to the following time-honored techniques of vigorous writing.

■**Write from the "me viewpoint."** Based on the premise that the best way to hold the reader's attention is to write from the writer's perspective, SlumberWrite is programmed to shift the focus of any message from the reader's interests and concerns to the writer's. SlumberWrite will change, for example, a reader-centered sentence, "The enclosed brochure will tell you everything you need to know about our services," to a writer-centered sentence, "Enclosed is a brochure listing our services and fees." Likewise, SlumberWrite will alter "So you can receive a full refund, please send your receipt" to "We cannot refund your money unless you send your receipt."

■**Organize your message into long, rambling paragraphs.** Because research shows that most business writing is read in a leisurely fashion and without interruption, SlumberWrite promotes a thoughtful, deliberate style by rejecting paragraphs with fewer than seven sentences. Also purged are techniques such as organizing material under clear topic sentences (as in "Our customers expressed three major concerns. First, . . .") and linking paragraphs with transitional words and expressions (as in "Therefore, . . ." and "Despite these problems, . . .").

■**Avoid variety in sentence structure and length.** The underlying principle here is monotony. Readers love it. Because SlumberWrite considers all stylistic embellishment frivolous, it will not permit cheap tricks such as following a long, complex sentence with a simple, short one. Subordination, which directs the reader's attention to the main clause, is strictly prohibited.

SlumberWrite, for example, would revise the preceding paragraph to: "The underlying principle here is monotony. Readers love monotony. SlumberWrite considers stylistic embellishment frivolous. It will not permit cheap tricks. An example of a cheap trick is to follow a long, complex sentence with a simple, short one. Subordination directs the reader's attention to the main clause. So subordination is strictly prohibited."

■**Use wordy expressions and tired, worn-out language.** SlumberWrite will ensure that you haven't used a flimsy expression when a meatier one is called for. It is programmed, for example, to replace "until" with "until such time as," "during" with "during the course of," and "if" with "in the event that." In addition, SlumberWrite will insert at regular intervals such old-time favorites as "As per your request," "Please be advised," and "I look forward to hearing from you at your earliest convenience."

■**Noun your verbs and verb your nouns.** Writing with nominalizations, or the noun form of verbs and adjectives, is a proven method for slowing your pace and avoiding the embarrassment of straightforward communication. SlumberWrite will alter presumptuous declarations such as "I recommend" and "Please consider" to more cautious statements such as "My recommendation is" and "Please take under consideration." Conversely, SlumberWrite eschews perfectly good verbs such as "discuss" and "meet" in favor of verbed nouns such as "dialogue" and "conference," as in "Let's dialogue about this" and "We need to conference on that."

Anything as revolutionary as SlumberWrite is bound to seem outlandish to some, but consider this: Verb Those Nouns, Inc., is so confident of its product that it will fly you at its own expense to an undisclosed test site.

There you can observe first-hand the effect of this spectacular new software package: managers snoozing at their desks, their heads buried in piles of unread reports; secretaries slumped over keyboards, their eyes glazed in trancelike lethargy; prospective customers overcome by torpor, their minds so dazed that they are unable to comprehend a single brochure or sales letter.

Take my word for it. It's an awe-inspiring sight.

Speaking English as It Was Meant To Be Spoken

It's a crazy, mixed-up world.

I mean, it used to be men were men, and women were women. Men had careers and supported their families, and women stayed home and took care of the children. That's the way it's supposed to be. And now look. You've got men staying home and women working. Not only that, but now women are demanding equal wages for equal work. I ask you: Where's the logic in that? I just don't get it.

I've noticed the same kind of craziness in the way we use language. English is the greatest language in the world. I don't see why people want to be messing with it.

I'll give you some examples.

People these days are beginning their sentences with "and" or "but." They think it gives their writing a conversational tone. Can you believe it? Even the new American Heritage Dictionary questions the rule against starting sentences this way. It says the rule has been ridiculed by grammarians such as Follett and Fowler and ignored by writers from Shakespeare to Woolf.

Now that really burns me. If you can't trust dictionaries not to change, whom can you trust? Next thing you know they'll be adding new words such as "fax."

Same thing with split infinitives. People are writing "to clearly understand" and "to really like you" rather than "clearly to understand" and "really to like you." They claim they should be able to put their adverbs where they want as a matter of emphasis. Now don't tell me how for hundreds of years the split infinitive was considered perfectly acceptable and how it wasn't until the 19th century that grammarians started saying it was wrong, because I don't want to hear it.

And what about prepositions? People are ending their sentences with them right and left. They're writing ''Who should I send the memo to?'' rather than ''To whom should I send the memo?'' I don't care what William Zinsser and Joseph Williams say in their books about the importance of using natural-sounding language. They can take their natural-sounding language and go be natural with someone else, as far as I'm concerned.

Those guys worry too much about what the reader thinks. Who cares what the reader thinks? It should be ''To whom should I send the memo?'' and that's the end of it. Those modern writing experts. They make me sick.

And don't tell me it's all right to write a one-sentence paragraph either.

When I went to school, I was taught a paragraph had three parts. How can you introduce your topic, develop it, and offer a resolution in a single sentence? You can't, that's how.

Now you've got those business writers writing one-sentence paragraphs. What do they think they're doing? Trying to create special emphasis? I'll tell you what they're doing: They're begging for the reader's attention. They ought to just leave him alone.

You heard me. I said ''him.'' In *The Handbook of Nonsexist Writing*, Miller and Swift say I should use ''him or her'' or switch the pronouns to the plural, but I won't do it. And don't tell me those newfangled words such as ''mail carrier'' for ''mailman'' and ''committee chair'' for ''committee chairman'' are just as good as the old ones, because they're not.

Messing with the language. It makes me sick. I don't even want to think about it.

Humor Can Take You Far— Sometimes Too Far

People with a good sense of humor make good bosses. They also make good communicators, good colleagues, and good friends. They can be a lot of fun to be around. They can also try your patience.

Take me, for example. Sometimes I'm funny, and sometimes I'm—well, I guess it depends on your definition of "humor."

Most people would agree that humor is a powerful tool of communication. It helps us connect with each other. It reminds us that we are human.

In business writing, the most effective humor tends to be subtle and low key. It is often no more than a cleverly turned phrase or a surprising choice of words. A manager, for example, might gently reject a staff member's ill-conceived recommendation by calling it "creative."

Paradoxically, humor is sometimes the writer's best tool for making a serious point. A brochure published jointly by the Bemidji Area Cross-Country Ski Club and the Bemidji Visitor & Convention Bureau uses humor in offering this safety tip:

"Use extra caution when skiing in areas where ski trails and snowmobile trails intersect, and avoid skiing on trails marked for snowmobiling. They [snowmobilers] cruise with delight at alarming speeds and a chance encounter with a slow-moving skier could prove to be unhealthy. In addition, they pay for and work on their own trails and are entitled to pedestrian-free snowmobiling."

The message could have been delivered with stone-face solemnity. Instead, the brochure makes a playful appeal to the reader's common sense. The playfulness not only adds emphasis to the warning but also prepares the reader for what comes next, a serious reminder of snowmobilers' rights.

Despite its power for bringing people together, humor can also create distance. What is funny to one person may be offensive to another. And then there is always the risk that some readers won't get it.

Take this column as an example. A few months ago I decided to do something on how to write vigorously, except instead of giving straight advice I did it tongue-in-cheek. I recommended things like organizing your message into long, rambling paragraphs and avoiding variety in sentence structure and length. Just for fun, I also made up a name, SlumberWrite, for a fictitious software program that was guaranteed to "slumberize" your text.

Well, believe it or not, half a dozen readers have written to ask me where they can get their hands on this amazing new program. I don't know. It makes you wonder.

Then a couple weeks ago I decided to impersonate the angry voice you sometimes hear from people who don't want language to change, so I pretended to rail against writers who begin their sentences with "and" or "but" and who use new words such as "fax." My point, of course, was that language does change and that certain changes are necessary and good.

Well, I heard from dozens of readers agreeing with every point I had jokingly espoused. My favorite letter, though, came from Patricia Christensen of Las Vegas, who suspected I was kidding but didn't want to take any chances:

"Please tell me that this article was written 'tongue in cheek'—tell me it was a joke—tell me you are a master of satire.

"If the above isn't true—and this article was a representation of how you actually relate to the written word—I hope that your horse and buggy gets you where you want to go—I hope that your smoke signals reach those that you communicate with on a regular basis.

"*And finally I hope* that no on paid one ounce of attention to that unbelievable drivel, '*Who cares what the reader thinks?*'

"You can't be serious."

That's the problem with irony (and the risk of using humor in the work place). When people don't get it, they either love you or hate you for the wrong reasons.

Tricks of the Trade

Five Easy Lessons in Clear Thinking and Writing

Why is it that some people are able to convey their thoughts clearly in writing, while others are not? Why does language seem to come easily for a few naturally gifted writers, while the rest of us seem destined to struggle?

What makes the difference?

The answer is simple: brains. We might as well admit it. Clear writing is a matter of smarts. As H. L. Mencken told us years ago, most people "write badly because they cannot think clearly." The reason they cannot think clearly, he added, is that "they lack the brains."

The solution? Brain transplants. That's right. It used to be that, if you weren't satisfied with the brain you were born with, you were stuck. Nowadays, however, you can have a transplant. Most of the successful writers I know have had one.

Problem is, the operation is expensive, and it may entail disturbing side effects. Some people complain of marked changes in personality. Others worry that their new writing style, although clear, just doesn't seem natural. It isn't really *them*.

You may prefer, therefore, the more traditional method of training the brain you already have. Here's how you can learn to think more clearly, and in the process to write more clearly, in five easy lessons.

■**Word choice**. Clear writing is precise writing. If you and your co-workers are saddened or devastated by somebody's departure, don't write, "Your leaving will have an effect all of us." Choose words that best convey your true meaning, language that is specific, explicit, and appropriate to your audience. At the same time, show restraint. As Strunk and White advise in *The Elements of Style*, "Omit needless words." Unless you have a good reason for using a fancy word, use a plain one.

■**Sentence structure**. Short, simple sentences are easier to follow than long, complex ones. Generally, an overly long or complicated sentence can be improved simply by cutting it in two, particularly if the sentence has two main clauses joined with the conjunction "and" or if it has a dependent clause linked to the main clause by the pronoun "which." On the other hand, don't overdo it. Too many short sentences produce a choppy, broken style, just as too many long sentences produce a monotonous, boring style. Variety is the key. It creates a natural flow that helps hold your reader's interest.

■**Support**. One of the most empowering phrases in the English language is "for example." Explain your meaning with illustrations. Support your points with examples, facts, and stories. Instead of stopping with a statement such as "She is very dedicated and works hard," offer some concrete detail, as in "For example, she stayed until 8 o'clock three nights last week to help us complete this project on time." As Conrad and other writers have advised: Don't just *tell* the reader; *show* the reader.

■**Paragraph structure**. The best advice here again comes from Strunk and White: Make the paragraph your basic unit of composition. If your paragraphs are well organized and carefully developed, your writing probably will be clear. Not every paragraph needs to be written according to the conventional three-part structure. But when you think you're in trouble, go back to the basics: topic sentence, development, resolution.

■**Organization**. A good argument forms a coherent progression in thought. Present your points in logical order. Be direct and straightforward in your approach. One standard format, analogous to the three-part paragraph structure, is to lead off with your purpose statement (unless you are communicating bad news and you need a buffer). Next provide background information or a summary of your main points. Then conclude with your action statement or steps for implementation.

There you have it: five easy lessons in how to think and write clearly. Give them a try. They cost less than a brain transplant, and the side effects are minimal.

How Writing Can Help You Prepare a Terrific Speech

How would you define the perfect speaker?

As someone who holds your interest? As someone who entertains you or makes you laugh? As someone who has something important to say and says it with conviction? As someone who knows where he or she is going with the speech and moves through the material effortlessly?

Are you more affected by a speaker's style or content?

According to Bert Decker in *The Art of Communicating*, the key ingredient is "believability" because "No matter what is said, it is not going to make much difference in the mind of the listener unless a person is credible and believed. There can be no action where there is not belief and agreement."

How, then, does one achieve "believability"?

Is it merely a matter of mastering what Decker calls the "nine behavioral skills to effective interpersonal communication" (solid eye communication, good posture, natural gestures, appropriate dress and appearance, voice and vocal variety, effective use of language and pauses, active listener involvement, effective use of humor, and being your natural self)?

Public speaking is typically taught by focusing on these or related skills as the building blocks to success. Learn these techniques step-by-step, avoid the obvious   pitfalls of "eye darts," "slow blinks," distracting gestures, and annoying "umms," "ers," and "ahs," and you too can be a great speaker. Right?

Well, it's all good advice. But in our preoccupation to perfect style and delivery, don't we sometimes overlook the most important ingredient of all: language?

What better way is there to achieve believability than to be swept away by the enthusiasm that comes from conviction and confidence based on carefully chosen language? Or as Wendell Berry might ask, how better to achieve authenticity and connection than "standing by words"?

Here, then, is an approach to preparing speeches that puts writing front and center.

First, use writing as a method of exploration, or what scholars call a mode of inquiry. Writing provides a natural means of focusing and sharpening your thoughts, so use the writing process to your advantage. Get to know your topic by jotting down your questions and ideas, by writing around the points that intrigue or trouble you, by keeping a journal, or by summarizing your conclusions in a note to a colleague or a letter to a friend.

Next, organize your material into an outline. Then work on your delivery by writing a draft in what William Tacey, author of *Business and Professional Speaking*, calls an "oral style," which you can achieve by writing what you speak aloud to your imagined audience.

Now, set aside your draft and write another one. Keep doing this until the words come naturally and fluently. This is better than memorization, which involves returning repeatedly to the same rigid text until you have it by heart. Instead, this involves creating variations of an evolving text. With each pass through your material, you become more comfortable with choosing your wording as you seek to articulate and illustrate your thought, much as you will do when you actually deliver your speech.

Finally, use writing to create a safety net. Assuming that you don't plan to recite your speech from memory or to read it from a manuscript (both methods make natural delivery nearly impossible), you will be working from brief notes, so give yourself a break. Write out, word for word, your key passages (introduction, transitions, and conclusion), so you *can* resort to reading if you begin to falter. Knowing that you have these polished gems in reserve can be tremendously comforting, both to the novice and the expert.

So, whatever your purpose—whether to inform, to instruct, to stimulate, to entertain, or to persuade (the five most common purposes in speaking)—you are more likely to be successful if you make writing part of your preparation.

"Elegant Variation" Is an Affectation To Avoid

Have you ever found yourself writing about a topic that required you to repeat the same word so many times you began to feel sorry for your reader?

What did you do?

If you're like many business writers, you probably looked for a synonym, a word with nearly the same meaning as the word you were trying to avoid repeating. After all, the reader appreciates variety, right?

The problem is that in attempting to solve one problem you may have created another. You may have provided variety at the expense of clarity. This error is so common that it even has a name: "elegant variation."

And yes, as you might have suspected, it's worse than inelegant consistency.

Let's take an example. Let's say your profession is marketing research. You're an expert, a real pro at analyzing markets and trends. Your client is paying you big bucks for your expert advice on the marketability of a new product idea. Thumbs up, your client sinks a million into bringing the product to market. Thumbs down, your client holds off.

What do you do?

Like any good marketing expert, you identify the factors that will determine the product's success. Whether by telephone interviews, mail-in surveys, focus groups, or mall intercepts, you test those factors on a representative sample of prospective buyers.

When it comes time to write your report, you want to give it a little pizzazz, but you feel stuck with certain plain-sounding words: "customer," "buy," "product." Not only do you worry that your client will tire of the repetition, but after writing

150 similar reports in the last year, you could use a little variety yourself.

So you do what any well-intentioned, word-weary writer would do. You hit the thesaurus key and see what comes up: "buyer," "client," "consumer," "patron," "shopper," "acquire," "purchase," "commodity," "merchandise."

Now, instead of writing "Customers consider price the primary factor in their decision to use this product. A marginally higher price, however, would not decrease product use by long-term customers," you write, "Customers consider price the primary factor in their decision to buy this product. A marginally higher price, however, would not decrease commodity utilization by long-term consumers."

The elegant variation may offer variety, but it also creates ambiguity. Is "commodity utilization" the same as "product use," and are "long-term consumers" the same as "long-term customers"?

Likewise, you might cause confusion by substituting "respondents" for "participants," "purchasers" for "buyers," and "gauge" for "measure."

Here's another example. Compare this sentence and its variant:

■ "To be successful, a new product must offer customers benefits, and customers must consider those benefits important."

■ "To be successful, a new product must offer customers benefits, and customers must consider those advantages important."

In this case, elegant variation is linked to wordiness. Eliminating the unnecessary words solves both problems: "To be successful, a new product must offer benefits that customers consider important." Or, perhaps better yet: "To be successful, a new product must offer customers important benefits."

There are times, of course, when word substitution is useful. Variety in word choice enlivens your writing. Consider this example: "Price appears to be the key factor among prospective buyers. Other factors are . . ." with "Price appears to be the key factor among prospective buyers. Other considerations are . . .''

Try reading both versions again out loud. Do you agree that the meaning of ''considerations'' is close enough to ''factors'' for it to serve as an acceptable, even desirable variation?

How can you tell when a substitution will work in your favor?

It's a matter of judgment, and sometimes it's a close call. But the question to ask is: Does the substitution offer variety in word choice without sacrifice in clarity or meaning?

My advice is, when in doubt, go for precision. After all, the pen may be mightier than the sword, but is the stylus more puissant than the scimitar?

Some Operating Principles that Apply to Writing

Woodrow Wilson thought his experience as President of Princeton University had provided him with invaluable training for his time in the White House. It was at the university, he once said, that he learned the art of politics, and from there he went to Washington to "practice among the amateurs."

I think I know what he meant.

Not that I've spent much time in the White House. In fact, other than a couple of guided tours, I've hardly spent any time there at all.

But I did work for 15 rewarding and exasperating years as a university administrator, and from that experience I learned just how political the job can be. Sometimes, on both good days and bad, I would turn to my favorite book on the subject and listen to a voice I always found to be calm, comforting, and reasonable: *The Effective Administrator* by Donald E. Walker.

In the conclusion of his book, Walker offers a series of observations or "axioms" reflecting his view of the world after a lifetime of service and leadership. Although these operating principles are intended for university administrators, they may be relevant to business managers as well. Here are some of my favorites:

■ "The university is filled with talented, sensitive human beings. Don't forget it. It is too easy to assume that people beneath you in the administrative structure are beneath you in other ways too."

■ "When problems become complicated, shorten the administrative lines. Get everyone concerned in the same room."

■ "Credit can and should be widely shared. Such sharing does not diminish individual accolades."

■"The secret cement of any organization is trust. Almost anything will work when enough trust is present. Without it, nothing works."

■"When you're wrong, admit it. Almost everyone will know it anyway. Your capitulation will be seen as reasonableness, not weakness."

■"Don't bully, threaten, or try to get even. Remember the words of Woody Allen: 'You can never get even with the world; it takes too long and too many lawyers.'"

Now, if Walker can distill so much humor, insight, and wisdom into so few words on effective management, why can't I do the same on effective writing? With that as my challenge, here's my list:

■Writing is a learnable skill. Forget the notion that some people are born writers and others are not. If you learn the basic rules and concentrate on certain principles, you can be a competent writer.

■Writing involves more than following rules. Correct writing is not always effective writing. Concentrate more on principles ("Good writing is concise writing") than on rules ("Never begin a sentence with 'Hopefully'").

■Writing is a sloppy process. Don't expect to write perfect copy in your first draft. As Ernest Hemingway said, "The only thing that matters about a first draft is that you finish it." Get it written, not right.

■Good writing is revised writing. Once you've written your first draft, take the time to revise it. Remember Samuel Johnson's observation: "What is written without effort is in general read without pleasure."

■Don't fall in love with your prose. Be open to the suggestions of others. Play around with alternate wording. Often a document can be improved by deleting even a good-sounding sentence or paragraph. Edit ruthlessly.

■There's more than one way to write effectively. When you make assignments to others, permit them to write in their own voice. Don't insist that every point of style conform to your way of doing things.

■For successful communication, you need to know three things: your audience, your purpose, and your material. Neglect any one of these, and you'll probably have problems.

■Good writing counts. Like it or not, there's a correlation between literacy and success, between communication skills and degree of influence. Writing is a skill worth developing.

There you have it: the world of work and writing according to Walker and Wilbers. Let me know if you think we've left anything out.

Verbing Your Nouns
and Nouning Your Verbs

As Calvin once said to Hobbes, "Verbing weirds language." I couldn't agree more. In fact, not only does verbing weird language but—of more consequence to business writers—nouning deads style.

Let me explain.

Like Calvin, I am fascinated by the process in which certain nouns and adjectives get verbed. Thirty years ago, for example, the noun "contact" was made into a verb, over the vehement objections of certain purists. Today we see the same thing happening to nouns such as "impact" and "access." They are getting verbed. Thirty years from now, few people will even remember that anyone objected.

Verbing language is a point worth discussing, so could we dialogue for a moment? Of course, as someone who instructions writing I would prefer to composition with you, but let's settle for a little conferencing.

Why do people like to verb their words?

For the same reason people wore powdered wigs in the eighteenth century and bell-bottoms in the 1960s. They think it makes them debonair or hip. Now I don't mean to argue that language should never change. Who would object, for example, to "fax" finding its rightful place in the English language, both as a noun and a verb? As our world—and our perception of it—changes, so must our language.

What I objection to is verbing words when doing so obscures rather than elucidates our meaning. If you'll interface with me on that, I think you'll agree. Hipping the language merely for the sake of hipping the language is neither perspicacious nor cool.

An even more serious threat to business writing is the reverse of verbing nouns: It is nouning verbs and adjectives, a process call nominalization, and it will dead your style faster than Superman can leap over a tall building.

Let me illustrate.

A basic formula for vigorous writing, according to Joseph Williams, is to make your sentences tell stories about characters. You do this by using your subjects to name characters and your verbs to name actions.

For example, "An investigation was conducted concerning our accounting procedures" merely states a fact, but "The IRS investigated our accounting procedures" tells a story by naming a character and an action. The noun "investigation" has less impact than the verb "investigated," particularly when the noun is linked to a nondescript verb, "conducted," and the verb is linked to a threatening character, "the IRS."

Here's another example. Compare "Attempts were made by the sales staff to achieve more efficient usage of their time" to "The sales staff attempted to use their time more efficiently." Can you hear the difference?

Now I'll give you the nominalized version and *you* change the noun to a verb to make the sentence tell a story: "My denial of your request was a necessity."

What did you come up with? Something like, "I had to deny your request"?

Here's another example: "There must be thorough preparation if you have a desire to make a presentation to the board."

Try: "You must prepare thoroughly if you want to speak to the board."

One more: "It is my belief that there should be a discussion of the reasons behind my decision regarding denial of your request for a paid leave."

In this case, change the sentence to "I would like to discuss why I denied your request for a paid leave," which leaves the last two nominalizations, "request" and "leave," as nouns.

In other words, nouning your verbs, like verbing your nouns, is not always wrong. There are times when it is necessary to bend your words to suit your needs. Both in writing and in speech, this is called inflection. Who could objection to that?

Writing on the Job

The Three-step Memo Gets the Job Done in a Pinch

If your experience with on-the-job writing is anything like mine, you know how easy it is to write a clear, concise memo.

All you have to do is request not to be interrupted for half an hour or so, close your office door, clear your mind of all distractions, sit in quiet reflection until your thoughts begin to crystallize, and capture the words as they flow effortlessly from your mind with perfect clarity and impeccable style. Right?

Well, maybe not.

The truth more often is this: As you try to get your thoughts down, you are distracted by dozens of competing concerns and preoccupations, including the co-worker in the hallway who is describing in intimate detail his marvelous mid-winter vacation in the Cayman Islands. A hour later, after two people have walked into your office and five people have called you on the phone—each needing an immediate response—you have completed your memo, which is supposed to be an articulate, organized, cogent statement of your purpose in writing.

So what's new?

The next time you find yourself trying to write a memo in less-than-ideal conditions like these, try organizing your thoughts using this simple, three-step formula: purpose, support, proposed action. It is more than a time-saver for you. It also ensures that you are stating your purpose clearly and getting to the point quickly for your reader.

Here's how it works.

Organize your message into three paragraphs beginning with these phrases:

"I am writing because (or to) . . ."
"The facts are . . ."
"I propose that you . . ."

Let's take some jumbled thoughts and give it a try: You have just received a memo from a vendor telling you that the delivery of software programs promised for February 15 will be at least one month late. What really annoys you is that you chose this particular vendor because he promised an early date. To show him he can't put you off like this, you'll threaten to invoke your contract's $1,000-a-day penalty clause.

Here's the memo, written according to the three-point formula:

"I am writing because I need our new software program installed and operational by February 15, as you promised it would be.

"The facts are that I accepted your bid over your competitors because you guaranteed the earliest delivery date. Now, I must hold you to your promise.

"I propose that either you complete installation by February 15 or I invoke the clause of our contract that provides for $1,000 penalty for each day past the deadline you take to complete the project."

After you have written your first draft using these three cues, you may want to go back and change your lead sentences to make them suit your style. But the approach still works because it's nearly impossible to complete the phrases without directly stating your purpose, the circumstances, and the action you are calling for.

If you find this method useful, you may want to create a macro on your word processor so that these cues (along with the current date, heading information, and your name) appear on command, thus relieving you of having to face that dreaded blank screen.

The 3-step formula also works for very brief communications. Let's say you are leaving a recorded phone message or sending a quick note by e-mail. Take, for example, this urgent message, which follows the formula without using the actual cues: "I'm concerned about our Omaha office. Our sales these have plummeted 50 percent over the past two months. Please find out what's going on and report to me next Monday."

There it is: one, two, three.

I realize there's something distasteful about this mechanical, almost mindless approach to communication. Organizing your thoughts with the same standard phrases is a little like painting by the numbers. But when you need to crank out a clear, concise memo in a hurry, why start form scratch?

The Executive Summary and the One-Page Report

How long is long enough? That's one of the hardest questions to answer in business writing.

How long should my letter be? How long should my report be? How long should my proposal be? Should it be one page? Should it be 10 pages? Should it be 100 pages?

On one level, the answer is obvious: Your document should be as long as it takes to get the job done, and not one word longer.

But how long is that?

Depending on your purpose, your audience, and your material, that could be . . . well, that could be any of the above. But in the vast majority of cases, the answer is *one page or less*.

Consider your own experience. You have five minutes to read your mail before going to a meeting. You find six pieces in your tray. (We'll exclude electronic mail for now.) The first three pieces are one page each. The fourth is 18 pages. The next two are 3 pages each.

What do you do?

Assuming the documents are of equal importance, you read the three 1-page documents immediately. Next you skim the two 3-page documents. Finally you glance at the 18-page document. That's all the time you have for now.

At the end of the day you stuff the 18-pager, still unread, into your briefcase, promising yourself you will get to it after dinner, which of course you don't do. Over the next several days, the 18-pager becomes a faithful companion as it travels with you to and from the office. On some days it accompanies you to lunch. It may even go with you on vacation. Finally (again depending on its importance), you get around to reading it. By this time, however, you have accumulated another half dozen traveling behemoths, and you charge through the entire assemblage in one sitting to end the agony.

Ah, the joy of reading business writing. Is there any wonder we love it so?

Now, if you are the writer and if what you've got to say cannot possibly be condensed into fewer than 18 pages, you don't necessarily have to place your document at the end of the reading queue by presenting it in all its behemothian splendor. You *can* have it both ways.

How? With the executive summary. It's a handy device, invented expressly for these situations.

Here's how it works.

You state your major points in outline form: one, two, three. That's it. If your reader lacks the time or the inclination to read your entire document, at least you have a chance of communicating your crucial points.

One approach, recommended by Ritchie R. Ward in *Practical Technical Writing*, goes like this:

■**Step 1**:   State what the document is about ("a definition of the problem; a statement of the objectives; a reason for doing the work expressed in terms of new products or increased profits; a statement of the conclusions reached; a statement of the recommendations made").

■**Step 2**:   Comment on the document's significance and implications ("a definitive statement about the importance of the investigation, followed by an interpretive statement of results suggested by the facts").

■**Step 3**:   Identify the actions you are calling for ("a recommendation of who is to do what, when they are to do it, and how they are to do it").

A similar approach, of my own creation, follows a six-part format:

■**Step 1**:   State your purpose and provide a brief background statement.

■**Step 2**:   Briefly describe the problem or issue to be resolved.

■**Step 3**: Comment on the significance or impact of the problem.

■**Step 4**: State your proposed solution.

■**Step 5**: Identify any drawbacks to your solution (these often have to do with cost).

■**Step 6**: Enumerate the benefits of your solution.

Now, if you are wondering how long your executive summary should be, we need to talk.

Making Performance Reviews
Less of a Burden

Once every year most managers suffer the agony, or experience the joy, of writing performance appraisals. Consider your own situation. Can you imagine anything more bothersome? Can you imagine anything more satisfying?

Your answer, I suspect, depends on the quality of the performance of the person you are evaluating, as well as on the quality of your working relationship. Whatever your situation, whether your task is to commend or to criticize, things may go better if you follow these basic guidelines.

■**Keep good notes on both accomplishments and shortcomings**. The time to begin gathering evidence of a job well done or examples of inadequate performance is *not* when you sit down to write the appraisal. If you take detailed and specific notes throughout the year, you'll have a much easier time developing and supporting your evaluation.

■**Leave no surprises for the assessment**. Your staff members will be more likely to meet your expectations if they know throughout the year how you perceive their performance. There is little point in withholding praise or criticism until the annual review.

■**Talk as well as write**. It's good practice to meet with the person whose performance you are evaluating, either before or after writing your assessment. This enables both you and your employee to verify your perceptions and to correct any misunderstandings. One approach is to use a draft of the appraisal as the basis for your conversation. Any new information or inaccuracies that are identified in the meeting can then be reflected in the final draft.

■**Start and end with the positive**. People tend to be more open to criticism if you lead off by recognizing their accomplishments and if you conclude by expressing your confidence (or at least your hope) that they will perform successfully in the future.

■**Be specific when calling for change**. Describe any shortcomings in performance, and specify how your employees need to improve or change. If appropriate, identify the penalties for continued inadequate performance.

■**Be respectful when offering criticism**. In *How To Say It*, Rosalie Maggio offers advice on writing a letter of reprimand that is relevant here: "Your goal . . . is not to get revenge or blow off steam—it is to effect a change in employee behavior. The best way to do this is to be encouraging and respectful. Avoid condemning, belittling, haranguing, preaching, scolding, or patronizing."

■**Allow staff members to respond in writing**.   Whether your employees agree or disagree with your assessment, it's only fair that they be given a chance to enter an opinion into the record.

■**Invite staff members to assess *your* performance as a manager**.   This may seem bizarre to some (and threatening to others), but more and more managers are making performance appraisals a two-way street. In "When Workers Rate the Boss" (in the March 1993 issue of *Training*), Robert McGarvey and Scott Smith offer an amusing anecdote: "After six straight box-office flops, movie mogul Samuel Goldwyn knew he had a problem, but he didn't know where. So he decided to ask those who should know: his underlings. 'I want you to tell me what's wrong with me and MGM,' he ordered, 'even if it means losing your job.'"

Now that you know how to go about preparing for and conducting a performance appraisal, you're ready to write. If your company does not provide you with a standard format, you may find it helpful to organize your review under these categories:

■Regular job duties (based on job description)
■Special assignments and miscellaneous projects
■Service and professional development
■Working relations

■Communication skills.

If you still have trouble writing performance appraisals, remember your employees' perspective: At the end of a long, hard year, the most concrete measure of their contributions may be your carefully compiled, thoughtfully composed record of their accomplishments—that and a handsome raise.

"Adequate" Not Adequate in Performance Reviews

How many times have you found yourself in this situation? You have been asked to evaluate an employee's performance. The employee's performance is adequate. It's not outstanding, and it's not awful. It's adequate.

Nothing wrong with that, but when you try to find a word that accurately reflects your assessment, you begin to feel uncomfortable. The employee's performance falls somewhere between exemplary and deficient, but none of the words describing that vast middle ground—"adequate," "satisfactory," "sufficient," "acceptable"—seems quite right.

The reason for your struggle may have more to do with the quirkiness of language than with the sensitive nature of performance evaluations. That's because, depending on their context, words can have more than one meaning.

Consider, for example, the contrary meanings of "unqualified" in these two sentences: "Your report was an unqualified success," meaning absolute and total, and "The applicant was unqualified," meaning insufficient, unfit, and below expectations.

Although the contrast in meaning is less pronounced, "adequate" has the same double quality. Like "satisfactory," "adequate" can mean either "completely sufficient" or "barely sufficient." When applied to quantity, as in "Our cash reserves are adequate," the word seems unconditional; there is no need for a larger quantity. But when applied to a personal quality, as in "Your performance is adequate," the word seems conditional; expectations have been met, but only barely.

Oddly enough, you can hear both meanings in this sentence: "An adequate performance is not adequate."

Perhaps this is why auditors are perplexed when their readers respond negatively to language such as "In our opinion, as of our audit date, the internal accounting and operating controls over inventory and quality assurance are adequate." What the quantity-minded auditors intend as approval is often taken by their quality-minded readers as disapproval, a less-than-satisfactory rating.

Perhaps what we need is a category describing performance that is worse than "adequate" but better than "unsatisfactory." How about "mediocre"? Now there's a word you can get your hands around. It comes from Latin, *mediocris*, which comes from two words, *medius* meaning middle and *ocris* meaning a rugged mountain. The literal meaning is "halfway up a rugged mountain."

Now, if you're only halfway up a rugged mountain, you're definitely not there. If your performance is "mediocre," it's clearly below expectations. No ambiguity there. Too bad "mediocre" is such a harsh-sounding word.

Another solution might be to adopt the British usage of "quite," as in "quite adequate" or "quite satisfactory." "Quite" in this usage has a peculiar, purgative effect: It eliminates the negative element from the word it modifies. "Quite adequate" means more than just "adequate." It means everything desired, completely adequate. Unfortunately, "Your performance is quite adequate" sounds imprecise to the American ear.

The real problem, of course, is human nature. Most of us just plain don't like being told we're average. We want to be excellent, outstanding, wonderful. The inescapable reality, however, is that most of us *are* average.

My solution?

Change human nature. That's right. We need to start a campaign persuading people to accept their ordinariness, even rejoice in it. Garrison Keillor has the right idea when he talks about those average Minnesotans in Lake Wobegon.

Until this campaign takes hold, however, I suggest we simply avoid loaded words such as "adequate" and instead use slightly inflated words such as "good."

A simple three-point scale might be: "outstanding," "good," and "needs improvement." For a five-point scale, I recommend: "outstanding," "commendable," "satisfactory," "marginal," and "unacceptable." To avoid the ambiguity of "satisfactory," you could eliminate that category and use a four-point scale.

How To Make
Letters of Recommendation Work

There are many good reasons not to write a letter of recommendation. You may prefer to retain a hard-working and competent staff person in your own department or company. You may worry about getting sued for defamation.

There is also the question of usefulness. How reliable are these traditional forms of validation and credentialing, anyway? As the writer, how free are you to give a truly candid appraisal? As the reader, how can you be certain that you are getting a truthful evaluation? When, for example, was the last time you read one that contained anything negative about the subject?

For all their limitations, letters of recommendation *can* serve as important components in the job search. Here's how to make them work, from all three perspectives in the communication triangle: subject, author, and reader.

A good letter of recommendation begins with the subject. If you are the person for whom the letter is being written, you should:

■Query first. Give the person you are asking to write on your behalf the opportunity to decline. A hesitant or unwilling writer is unlikely to give you an enthusiastic recommendation.

■Make your request in a timely fashion. Try to give your writer two or three weeks' lead time. Last-minute requests are an imposition.

■Provide pertinent information (address, position title, and job description, if available) in writing. To help your writer be specific, you may want to provide a detailed summary of your accomplishments and work history.

■Coordinate the areas to be covered by the persons writing for you. Identify the writers to each other. Explain how their various perspectives might complement each other.

■Indicate whether you are waiving your right to read the letter, as guaranteed to you under the Privacy Act of 1974. Keep in mind that "closed" letters generally carry more weight than "open" letters.

■As a matter of courtesy, provide a stamped, addressed envelope and inform the person writing for you of the outcome.

Now, if you are the person writing the letter, you should:

■Know whether your company policy permits you to give references on current or former employees and respond accordingly.

■Consider declining if you are unable to provide an enthusiastic endorsement.

■Write your letter according to this five-part formula:

1. Clearly identify the person being recommended and the purpose of the recommendation. Make specific reference to the position in question.

2. Identify yourself and indicate how well you know the person being recommended.

3. Describe in specific detail the job duties of the person.

4. Offer an assessment of the person's skills, abilities, qualities, knowledge, and experience. Comment explicitly on how these points meet the particular qualifications for the position in question.

5. Provide a closing statement summarizing and reiterating your opinion of the person being recommended. Because the wording and tone of this final assessment carry special weight, choose carefully between phrases such as "well qualified" and "exceptionally competent," and between statements such as "I recommend Ms. Anderson for your consideration" and "Ms. Anderson has my enthusiastic and unqualified support for this position."

Finally, if you are the person receiving the letter, you should:

■Seek assessments from additional references. Sometimes unsolicited assessments are the most revealing.

■Check with the previous employer, who has no vested interest in the outcome of the job search.

■Consider calling and talking with the author. Often people will be more candid when speaking.

■Question the motives of someone who seems too eager to let an employee go or who tells you, "My loss is your gain." What that usually means is, "My loss is your loss."

Doing it with Style!

To Improve Your Writing, Read (and Copy) Good Writers

As writers have known for centuries, the best way to learn to write well is to apprentice yourself to an accomplished writer.

Learning to write is like developing any other skill. You begin by imitating, point by point, someone who has mastered the basic techniques of the form. At first your style may sound derivative, but over time, as you experiment with applying those techniques, your own distinct voice emerges.

I remember the time the critic and editor Malcolm Cowley visited my creative writing class at Vanderbilt. After telling us stories about Fitzgerald, Wolfe, and Hemingway, he offered this advice: The next time you read something that you find compelling, a passage whose language seems extraordinarily well crafted, mark the passage, come back to it, and study it. Read it out loud. Copy or type it over word for word. Try to write something like it. In other words, do whatever you can to get as close as possible to the language that moved you.

In this way, he told us, you discover a writer's secrets and you make them your own.

A few years ago, when reading Toni Morrison's *Beloved*, I came across a passage that sent chills down my spine. It began, "The stove didn't shudder as it adjusted to its heat." Before I realized what was happening, Seth's haunted house was trembling and pitching, a table came rushing across the floor, and Paul D had grabbed it by its leg and was bashing it about, "wrecking everything, screaming back at the screaming house."

I have often marvelled at Morrison's uncanny ability to glide effortlessly between the natural and the supernatural worlds. How does she do it? I wanted to know.

I took Cowley's advice and copied and studied the passage. I took it apart and wrote another passage like it. Although I may never write like Morrison, I did learn something from the exercise.

You can take the same approach to improving your business writing. Let's give it a try.

We'll use an obvious example: Thomas J. Watson's famous 1970 memo to IBM managers castigating them for their use of "gobbledygook." His memo is a model of no-nonsense, forceful writing:

"A foreign language has been creeping into many of the presentations I hear and the memos I read. It adds nothing to a message but noise, and I want your help in stamping it out. It's called gobbledygook.

"There's no shortage of examples. Nothing seems to get finished anymore—it gets 'finalized.' Things don't happen at the same time but 'coincident with this action.' Believe it or not, people will talk about taking a 'commitment position' and then because of the 'volatility of schedule changes' they will 'de-commit' so that our 'posture vis-a-vis some data base that needs a sizing will be able to enhance competitive positions.'

"That's gobbledygook.

"It may be acceptable among bureaucrats but not in this company. IBM wasn't built with fuzzy ideas and pretentious language. IBM was built with clear thinking and plain talk. Let's keep it that way."

Let's concentrate on four specific points worth imitating. The first is structural. Notice how Watson organizes his memo into a logical, three-part sequence: purpose statement, support, and proposed action.

The other three points all have to do with techniques for creating emphasis: Watson's use of a one-sentence paragraph, the parallelism of the contrasting statements beginning with "IBM," and the short, punchy concluding sentence.

After you have copied or typed over his memo, write a memo on another topic that imitates, point by point, each of these attributes. Where Watson uses a one-sentence paragraph, you use a one-sentence paragraph. Where he uses parallel construction, you use parallel construction.

Remember, as Yoggi Berra once said, "You can observe a lot just by watching." To which I might add, you can accomplish a lot just by doing.

Variety in Sentence Structure Invigorates Writing

There are few things more beautiful than a simple declarative sentence.

Take, for example, what is arguably the most beautiful sentence in the English language: "I love you." What accounts for its beauty and power? Is it its thought? Is it its simplicity? Is it its uncanny ability to elicit the most complex of human emotions in the most elemental of language?

"I love you" dramatically illustrates the potency of simple words and direct communication. Subject, verb, object. Structure and content seem perfectly suited.

But what happens when this simple, straightforward sentence is followed by a series of others like it? "I love you. You love me. Do you like music? We could be three."

Well, obviously, something is lost. What was admirable is now trite. What was evocative is now pedestrian. One simple sentence after another becomes too much of a good thing. In business writing as in life, the reader wants variety.

Here is a paragraph that illustrates the problem of writing without variety: "Our company is named Northwoods Industries. It was founded in 1972. It now employs 319 people. Approximately 60 percent of these people are unskilled or semi-skilled laborers. These laborers work on assembly lines. Another 25 percent are engineers. These technicians design our products. The remaining 15 percent are managers. These professionals worry about the bottom line. They also try to create a team atmosphere."

Monotonous sentence structure reflects a failure of imagination. The author of the preceding paragraph simply listed the information in the most obvious sentence units, without bothering to vary the sentence structure and length.

The monotony created by writing in unbroken strings of simple declarative sentences can be avoided by employing a basic writing technique called *subordination*. This involves making independent clauses (sentences that stand alone) into dependent units (phrases or clauses that must be attached to independent clauses, often with commas marking their juncture).

For example, the first three sentences, all of which have the same subject, might be condensed into a single sentence: "Founded in 1972, Northwoods Industries now employs 319 people." Not only does the subordinated dependent phrase, "founded in 1972," allow for more succinct expression, but it also introduces an element of variety into the flow of the language.

The next four sentences can be condensed in similar fashion, by subordinating the second and fourth sentences and attaching them to the first and third sentences: "Approximately 60 percent of these people are unskilled or semi-skilled laborers who work on assembly lines. Another 25 percent are engineers who design our products." Although some repetition in sentence structure remains, it now works to the writer's advantage by building momentum.

Too much repetition, however, creates monotony. This can be avoided by combining the last three sentences, "The remaining 15 percent are managers. These professionals worry about the bottom line. They also try to create a team atmosphere," into a single sentence: "The remaining 15 percent are managers who not only worry about the bottom line but also try to create a team atmosphere."

The revised paragraph reads: "Founded in 1972, Northwoods Industries now employs 319 people. Approximately 60 percent of these people are unskilled or semi-skilled laborers who work on assembly lines. Another 25 percent are engineers who design our products. The remaining 15 percent are managers who not only worry about the bottom line but also try to create a team atmosphere."

For practice, you might want to play around with these basic sentence types:

Simple: "I will vary my sentence structure."

Compound: "I will vary my sentence structure, and I will write in a more vigorous style."

Complex: "If I vary my sentence structure, I will write in a more vigorous style."

Compound-Complex: "I want to write in a more vigorous style because I want to be successful, and I will succeed."

Have fun.

"How Can I Learn To Write with Style?"

"I want to be more than a competent writer. I want to be more than a clear writer. I want to be a *good* writer. I want to be a colorful and engaging and memorable writer. How can I learn to write with style?"

The first time I heard those words (from an undergraduate in a literature class I was teaching at the University of Iowa), it warmed my heart. Now, 20 years later, when I hear similar declarations from people writing on the job, it warms my heart still.

It's what every teacher longs to hear. Teach me more than the bare minimum. I want to do more than just get by. I want to excel. Help me learn to write with style.

Where does one begin?

Well, it may seem paradoxical, but the best way to develop your style is to relax. Don't try too hard. As Strunk and White advise in *The Elements of Style*, approach style "by turning resolutely away from all devices that are popularly believed to indicate style—all mannerisms, tricks, adornments. The approach to style is by way of plainness, simplicity, orderliness, sincerity."

William Zinsser, whose "articles of faith" or "cardinal goals of good writing" are clarity, simplicity, vitality, and humanity, recommends the same approach when he tells us, "You have to strip down your writing before you can build it up."

With this in mind, here are my thoughts on style:

■**Write simply and clearly**. A good writing style is one that enhances rather than detracts from the writer's message. To achieve clear communication, Patricia Westheimer advises, "Write the way you speak—conversationally and naturally." As Beth Luey explains in *Handbook for Academic Authors*, good writing "is clear and succinct. If you can move beyond clarity to grace and elegance, you are to be congratulated. Your editor will happily settle for clarity, however.''

■**Use concrete and specific language**. Word choice is key to style or the effect the writer has on the reader. You can make a more definite impression by using words that capture and reflect your meaning precisely, as in ''We were devastated by the news'' rather than ''We were affected by the news.'' As a rule, prefer nouns and verbs over adjectives and adverbs, as in ''I recommend that we improve our marketing'' rather than ''It is my recommendation that we improve our marketing effort.''

■**Vary your sentence structure and length**. A fundamental rule of style is that variety is interesting, monotony boring. Variety adds energy and life to your writing. Avoid the monotony that comes from writing one simple declarative sentence after another, beginning every sentence with a subordinate clause, or writing in pairs of sentences joined with the conjunction ''and.'' Similarly, vary your sentence (and paragraph) length. For particular emphasis, try following a long sentence with a short sentence or even a fragment. Like this.

A one-sentence paragraph can have the same effect.

■**Read and copy good writers**. The more you read, the more likely you will improve your style. To take a more intentional approach, keep a file of good writing samples—the best memo or letter or report you've ever read—and browse through your file from time to time to remind yourself of what you liked about each sample. Style involves technique or manipulation of words, sentences, and paragraphs. You can learn what works from the masters.

Remember: Style comes as much from practice as from conscious effort. If you are writing with a few basic principles of good writing in mind, your style will develop naturally over time.

More than a hundred years ago the English critic and essayist Matthew Arnold offered this advice: ''People think I can teach them style. What stuff it is. Have something to say and say it as clearly as you can. That is the only secret of style.''

Adapt Your Style To Fit the Audience, Occasion

How do you define a great communicator?

Is it someone who:

■Conveys information clearly?

■Moves and inspires us?

■Gives voice to our deepest anxieties and our loftiest aspirations?

■Speaks and writes with style?

■Adapts style to the audience and situation?

If I had to choose just one, it would be the last. Great communicators are people who know the hearts and minds of their audience, who comprehend the nuances of a situation, and who adapt their tone and approach accordingly.

This requires the ability to speak and write in more than one voice. No matter how attractive or successful a particular style might be, according to John Fielden, "There is no one style of writing in business that is appropriate in all situations and for all readers, even though managers and subordinates usually talk and behave as if there were."

In other words, a style that is, say, personal and warm or one that is direct and forceful—traits typically associated with effective business writing—may be just the *wrong* style in certain situations.

How do you know which style is appropriate for which occasion?

As Fielden points out in "What do you mean you don't like my style?" (*Harvard Business Review*, May-June 1982), the choice is often determined by the writer's relationship to the reader (or the "power positions of both writer and reader"). He defines six basic styles and explains how to use them according to the audience and the situation.

■**Forceful style**—"usually appropriate only in situations where the writer has the power, such as in action requests in the form of orders or when you are saying no firmly but politely to a subordinate." Use the active voice—as in "Correct this error immediately" instead of "A correction should be made." Write in simple declarative sentences in subject-verb-object order without "putting namby-pamby phrases before the subject"—as in "I have decided to fund your project" instead of "After much deliberation and weighing of the pros and cons, I have decided to fund your project."

■**Passive style**—"often appropriate in negative situations and in situations where the writer is in a lower position than the reader." Avoid the imperative ("never give an order"); use "weasel words," long sentences, and "heavy paragraphs"; and write in the passive voice—as in "Valuable resources are being wasted" instead of "You are wasting valuable resources."

■**Personal style**—"usually appropriate in good-news and persuasive action-request situations." Use the active voice, short sentences "that capture the rhythm of ordinary conversation," contractions, direct questions to the reader, persons' names, and personal pronouns—especially "you" and "I," as in "I so much appreciate the work you've done" as opposed to "The work you've done is appreciated."

■**Impersonal style**—"usually appropriate in negative and information-conveying situations" and "always appropriate in technical and scientific writing." Avoid persons' names and personal pronouns, make some of your sentences complex and some paragraphs long, and use the passive voice "to make yourself conveniently disappear when desirable"—as in "An error in the calculations has been made" instead of "I think your calculations are wrong."

■**Colorful style**—sometimes "appropriate in good-news situations" and "commonly found in the highly persuasive writing of advertisements and sales letters." Insert adjectives and adverbs and use metaphors or similes—as in "Our solution strikes at the very *root* of Acme's problems."

■**Less colorful style**—"appropriate for ordinary business writing." Avoid adjectives, adverbs, metaphors, and figures of speech; blend the impersonal style with the passive style; and employ "words that remove any semblance of wit, liveliness, and vigor from the writing."

Apparently assuming that most of us are naturally gifted at writing colorlessly, Fielden offers no examples of this style.

The Kudos File

Touching Letter Offers Good Reason To Say Thanks

One of the things I like about writing this column is hearing from my readers. Today, I received a letter that brought tears to my eyes.

It came from Wendy (Wiberg) Wustenberg of Farmington, Minnesota. She was responding to the column I wrote in December about my "kudos" file and how meaningful a simple thank-you note can be.

My kudos file is an assortment of notes and letters written to me over the years by friends and associates. Sometimes, when I'm having a bad day, I thumb through my kudos file to cheer myself up.

One of the samples I mentioned was a note written to me 10 years ago by a staff member at the University of Minnesota (where I was then directing a student services unit that included academic advising). The staff member's supervisor had received a thank-you letter from a student advisee. When her supervisor forwarded the thank-you letter to me, I in turn forwarded it to the deans, some of whom wrote notes of appreciation to the staff member, who then wrote a note thanking me for taking the time to recognize her effort.

Well, in response to my column, Ms. Wustenberg of Farmington wrote to tell me that *she* was the student who wrote the thank-you letter that got all this started.

Here's her story, 10 years later:

"Yesterday my mother forwarded a photocopy of [one of your columns] with a very cordial message attached. She had already thanked several neighbors and family friends for drawing the column to her attention. At the center of this continuing thank-you chain was your mention of a long-ago thank you I evidently wrote to a University professor [actually, it was to a degree program adviser in the College of Liberal Arts].

"My own file is a hodge podge of message slips, Post-it-notes, letters, and scribbles on the backs of envelopes. Each one has encouraged me to be more generous in turn, and it's true that acknowledgements such as yours warm the heart greatly and inspire even more notes.

"I'd like to share one personal story to add to your file of examples. During my years as the documentary producer at Twin Cities Public Television I mentored well over three dozen college interns. After each broadcast I tried to find time to jot notes to them—nothing special, just some acknowledgement of their hours of volunteer work.

"The University of Minnesota referred Dave Eckberg to me in the winter of 1987. He was undisciplined and somewhat unreliable in the early months. We survived some rocky projects and by the broadcast of the spring documentary I was seeing definite talents. My last note to him was quite a bit longer than usual because of our tumultuous history, and then we lost touch.

"In 1990 I received word that Dave had died of cancer and that the family wanted to invite me to the funeral. I was touched but also taken aback to be included at such a deeply personal time. The mystery was solved by Dave's father, who drew me aside and said that the thank-you note was still in a lock box in his son's room. He wanted to let me know that it was among Dave's most important possessions, and he thanked me for helping his son. We both stood there with tears running down our faces, and I realized for the first time how much these seemingly little gestures touch other people . . .

"I am [now] home raising a two-year-old and preparing for our second child to arrive. Being a mother has its own rewards, but your indirect kudos to me also came at a very good time. Thank you again."

Thank *you*, Ms. Wustenberg, for continuing this remarkable chain of human kindness. Who knows when it will end or where else it might lead?

Handwritten Notes of Appreciation Create Goodwill

When was the last time you sent a handwritten note to an employee or associate expressing your appreciation for a job well done?

If it has been more than a week, it's time for you to get back on schedule. If it has been more than a month, it's time for you to review how you are managing your time. If it has been more than a year, it's time for you to examine your style of management.

Sending a note of appreciation is an invaluable method of maintaining morale and creating goodwill. It requires little time and effort. In fact, it is perhaps the easiest writing a manager can do. The message is disarmingly simple: ''I appreciate your contribution.'' The only real requirement of the writer is thoughtfulness.

When is a note of appreciation called for? Consider writing one to recognize:

■**Contributions crucial to your mission.** A good way to encourage people to stay on task is to recognize those achievements you consider most significant to your goals or mission.

■**Performance reflecting commitment and dedication.** Whether the consequences are big or small, any behavior that reflects a person's loyalty or commitment merits recognition.

■**Achievements that might otherwise go unrecognized.** Sometimes the little things count the most. Your attention to the details of someone's day-to-day activities will communicate that you care.

■**Actions reflecting thoughtfulness and consideration.** A good way to raise someone's sensitivity is to thank that person for being sensitive. A good way to encourage thoughtfulness is to thank someone for being thoughtful.

Here are a few tips for writing your notes:

■**A written compliment carries more weight than a spoken one**. Even a hastily scrawled note conveys your appreciation more effectively than a spoken compliment. Not only does it require slightly more effort and thought on your part, but it becomes a record of your appreciation.

■**Timing is critical**. The sooner you recognize someone's contribution, the more genuine your appreciation will seem.

■**Your purpose should be limited to expressing appreciation**. Don't make the mistake of expressing your appreciation and requesting an additional contribution in the same communication. This diminishes the effect of your note and makes your appreciation seem insincere.

To illustrate how notes of appreciation might be written, I'll offer four examples. Two of these are effectively written, and two are not. Which ones work for you?

"Nice job. Your presentation at this morning's meeting was inspirational—hands down the best I've heard in months. I'm sure it will motivate every one of our sales reps."

"Thanks for making the coffee every morning. It's a chore no one likes to do, but you do it every day without complaining or grumbling. I really appreciate it. By the way, I noticed we're out of creamer. Could you pick some up on your way home from work tonight?"

"I appreciate the way you came to my defense yesterday. Jerry's accusation caught me by surprise. If you hadn't spoken up on my behalf, I'm afraid I would have responded defensively. It's reassuring to know that I can count on your support and honesty."

"I don't care what everybody says about you. I think you're a nice person."

The last one, of course, is my favorite.

Here's my challenge for you: Send a handwritten note of appreciation to at least one employee or associate every week for the next two months. Try to find someone who doesn't know you're watching or who doesn't think you care. The idea is to catch that person doing something right—then record your appreciation.

The Big Picture

Avoid Common Errors
When Writing Internationally

The spoiled American.

When it comes to international commerce and travel, we expect our counterparts to speak English perfectly, yet relatively few of us have mastered a foreign language ourselves.

We laugh when we hear of the Bangkok dry cleaner's sign that urges passers-by, "Drop your trousers here for best results," or of the Acapulco hotel that reassures its guests, "The manager has personally passed all the water served here." (Well, you must admit, it *is* funny.)

But even when using our own language to communicate internationally, we native-English writers often give little thought to the problems we may be causing our foreign-language readers. Here, according to John Kirkman's article in *Text, ConText, and HyperText: Writing with and for the Computer*, are some examples of how an "unthinking" or "unmindful" writer may cause confusion.

■**Inconsistent use of terms.** Readers in any language expect consistency. Logic suggests that a variation in language signifies a variation in meaning. If the "unthinking" writer, for example, refers in one instance to the "CRT," in another to the "monitor," and yet another to the "screen," the reader will likely assume that the writer intends three different meanings.

Similarly, the writer may confuse the reader by using a variety of expressions, such as "key in the data," "input the data," "type in the data," and "enter the data," to signify a single function. Conversely, fuzzy words such as "enter" have multiple meanings: "Sometimes *enter* means 'type in'; sometimes it means 'press a key, to transmit to a program file the data you have just typed in'; sometimes it means 'both type in and transmit the data'; and sometimes it means 'move into' (as in 'enter Program A from System X').''

The solution: Choose the most precise, least ambiguous word or expression, and use it consistently.

■**Culture-bound references.** Although cultural references lend color and personality to our writing, they should be avoided when alluding to ideas or entities that are not universally recognized, or when writing to readers in countries or cultures in which the allusions do not exist. A playful reference to April foolery or to giving someone "the bum's rush," for example, may bewilder the reader who is struggling to arrive at a literal understanding of the language.

■**Colloquial expressions.** Conversational language poses special difficulties for the non-native reader. Consider the potential misunderstanding created by a company whose slogan reads, "We understand your needs, because we've been there." "Been where?" the non-native reader is likely to ask.

Kirkman also points out the problematic use of "weasel words," such as "compromise" when used in place of "damage," as in "To ensure that you do not compromise your system's reliability" in place of "To avoid damaging your system's components."

■**Faux amis.** This French term, meaning "false friends," reminds us that look-alike words, such as "actually" in English and *"acutellement"* in French, sometimes have very different meanings. As a result, an expression such as "the actual program" is likely to be mistranslated by a French reader as "the current program." The thoughtful international writer will avoid the unnecessary use of English words that have *faux amis* in other languages.

■**British English and American English.** I remember my own experience in Colchester, England, where after five months as a Visiting Fulbright Fellow I thought I had pretty well acquainted myself with the differences between British English and American English. I had learned to say "lift" for "elevator," "lorry" for "truck," "dear" for "expensive," and "take a decision" for "make a decision." My young son and daughter were even beginning to speak with distinctly British accents (or— depending on your perspective—to lose their distinctly American ones).

You can imagine my discomfiture when on our last Sunday in England I walked down to the neighborhood bakery in Wivenhoe and asked for some "buns."

"Oh, sir," the young woman behind the counter said, blushing. "What you want are 'rolls.' We don't call them 'buns.'"

Who Gets the Blame
for Illiteracy in America?

My wife works part time registering and placing children in the Minneapolis school system. Often her work brings her into contact not only with children but also with parents who have difficulty reading and writing.

Once she was helping a mother fill out a form when she noticed something unusual. Under "marital status" the woman had written, "Two times a week."

By some standards, I guess, that's not so bad.

But the mother's inability to read and understand a common term such as "marital status" reflects a serious problem in American society.

According to a new government study, there are some 40 to 44 million Americans like her, adults who possess only the most rudimentary reading and writing skills. The "Adult Literacy in America" study also revealed that nearly half of all adult Americans read and write so poorly they have difficulty holding a decent job.

Who gets the blame for this shocking level of functional illiteracy in America?

You do. We do. The schools, the parents, the students— we all do.

It's a large problem, and we all bear some responsibility for it. High schools are awarding diplomas to students who can't read or write. Parents are spending too little time interacting with their children. And students are devoting too little effort to their number one responsibility in life—getting educated.

Who pays the price for functional illiteracy in America?

We all do, and ''we'' includes the business community, which for years has complained about poor writing skills among job applicants and new hires.

Shocking as it is, illiteracy is only part of the problem. Even among college graduates, even among those who write well, there are many ''well-educated'' people who are unable to perform the most basic business writing assignments, from formatting a simple memo to organizing a report or proposal.

''I remember the first time my boss told me, 'Put that in a memo,''' a young professional told me recently. ''I panicked. A memo? Of course I knew the term, but I had never seen or written one, either in high school or college, so I quickly went through the files in my office to see how they were done.''

It isn't that our educational institutions don't offer courses in business writing. The problem is that, for the most part, they don't teach basic business writing as an integral component of their writing instruction. Instead, business writing is considered a specialized skill necessary only for students in certain majors—even though most graduates will need these skills in their jobs and careers.

Reader Abby Farr-Petterson of Minneapolis raised this issue when she wrote: ''It seems to me that résumés, applications, memos, proposals, executive summaries, letters of request, and resignations are . . . crucial in getting and maintaining employment.

''My daughter will be using these 'business' forms as much as, and probably more than, the traditional academic writing still taught as the standard fare in the American High School. . . . If 'business writing' is offered in high school at all, it would be considered in the non-college preparation credit category by most colleges reviewing her transcript.''

Why is this? Why do many schools and educators persist in thinking of business writing as ''non-college preparation''? Why aren't basic business writing techniques taught as part of every college composition course? Why do we continue to emphasize writing as a literary or academic discipline to the exclusion of its practical applications? Why do we allow students to graduate from high school and college who have never read or written a memo?

Scholars have a new term to describe adults who know how to read but choose not to: ''aliterate.'' In some ways, aliteracy is as troubling a social problem as illiteracy.

Perhaps we need a new term for people who can write essays, book reports, and literature reviews but who haven't a clue about how to write position papers, weekly reports, and procedures.

How about ''biznilliterate''?

How Would You Grade Your Business Writing?

On a scale of 1 to 10, how good is your business writing?

Certain writers can answer that question precisely. Professional fund-raisers, for example, know how good their writing is to the penny. But they are the exception. Most of us have only a general sense of our effectiveness.

Here's a 10-point checklist that will give you a better idea of how you are perceived by your readers. I adapted it from a form used by the University of Minnesota's Carlson School of Management to evaluate the writing of its MBA students. Each item is worth one point.

■Opening
1. Clearly expresses writer's purpose/focus.
2. Stresses why the document is important to the reader (need/benefit).

■Body (analysis and development)
3. Develops ideas in logical, coherent sequence (with clear transitions and organized paragraphs).
4. Supports each main point with sufficient data (examples/illustrations, including tables and graphs where needed).

■Closing
5. Repeats benefits to reader.
6. States recommendation and action request.

■General Writing
7. Tone/Language is appropriate for audience.
8. Style is direct, assertive (prefers active, personal voice to passive, impersonal voice).
9. Text is highlighted (bullets, paragraphing, boldface, underlining, etc.) to engage reader and reinforce main points.
10. Copy is free of distracting errors in spelling, grammar, and punctuation.

I like this form because it breaks writing down into recognizable components, which are stated as positive goals or expectations. I also like that it can be used as a handy checklist by the writers themselves.

Scoring, however, is problematic. In an educational setting one can simply total up the points for grading and use the 10 items as the basis for discussion, coaching, and learning. But in the real world it doesn't work that way. As many business writers know, your on-the-job effectiveness is measured not in points but in success or failure. Your written document either works or it doesn't. It's an all-or-nothing world.

If your proposal is presented effectively, for example, your success more likely can be attributed to good execution of the first six items on the checklist. If, on the other hand, your proposal is ineffective, your failure more likely can be attributed to poor execution of the last four items.

In other words, certain components of effective writing count only when they're wrong. Furthermore, a single error of the wrong sort can outweigh all the positive elements combined. I call this "exponential deductibility."

Unfortunately, it gets worse than that. Certain errors, which again relate to the last four items, go beyond the scope of the document and the transaction at hand. These errors leave a residue of doubt regarding your credibility, causing the reader to make a negative assessment of your capability in all future transactions. Borrowing a phrase from Keats, I call this extra-textual phenomenon "negative capability."

One example of "negative capability" is using language that makes you appear arrogant or aloof ("Your letter is acknowledged" rather than "Thank you for your letter"). Another is writing in an impersonal style that makes you seem lethargic, apathetic, or passive ("A discussion is needed" rather than "We need to talk"). Similarly, a text devoid of any highlighting may go unread and, worse yet, may leave the reader with the impression that you are bland, boring, and predictable. And errors in spelling, punctuation, and grammar can make you seem ignorant, careless, and lacking in pride and professionalism.

It's a tough world, isn't it? But learning to identify the positive elements of effective writing while keeping in mind the twin pitfalls of ''exponential deductibility'' and ''negative capability'' might help you survive. You might even prosper.

The Book No Business Writer Should Be Without

"If you could own only one book on business writing," people often ask me, "which book would it be?"

Well, that depends on your particular interests and needs.

If, for example, you wanted a book that would give you timeless advice on style combined with reminders of how to avoid common errors in usage, I would recommend William Strunk Jr. and E. B. White's classic *The Elements of Style*. After decades in print, it's still the standard by which all other writing handbooks are measured. Professor Strunk and his one-time student White (also author of *Charlotte's Web*) offer excellent advice in a delightful style, laced with humor and wit.

Another excellent stylebook is Joseph Williams' *Style: Ten Lessons in Clarity & Grace*. I should warn you, however, that this book is not for the fainthearted. With good reason, Williams recommends that you work your way through the challenging exercises and lessons in "small chunks," one section at a time.

For an excellent discussion of the basic elements of good writing, combined with advice on particular types of writing such as interviews and sports, I would recommend William Zinsser's *On Writing Well*. A lively and entertaining writer, Zinsser often punctuates his advice with unforgettable quotes such as "Clutter is the disease of American writing" and "There's not much to be said about the period except most writers don't reach it soon enough."

On the other hand, if what you want is a good, basic handbook to help you avoid common writing errors such as lack of subject/verb agreement, dangling modifiers, and faulty parallelism, it's hard to do better than Edward P.J. Corbett's *The Little English Handbook*; and if what you want is a plain old reference book, *The Chicago Manual of Style* and William Sabin's *The Gregg Reference Manual* are hard to beat.

If you want to avoid sexist language in more sophisticated ways than merely writing "he or she," then Casey Miller and Kate Swift's *The Handbook of Nonsexist Writing* and Rosalie Maggio's *The Bias-Free Word Finder* are the books for you.

If getting started is your problem, you need Natalie Goldberg's *Writing Down the Bones*. Goldberg's practical, imaginative techniques are a sure antidote to writer's block. In the same spirit, Maggio in *How To Say It* will help you find the right word, phrase, sentence, paragraph, or sample letter to use in any one of 40 types of correspondence, from fund-raising letters to thank-you letters. Equally useful is Sherry Sweetnam's superb *The Executive Memo*, which presents models of business communication such as information memos and sales letters in a lively style and format.

And of course I know of someone who writes columns on effective business writing, but modesty prevents me from mentioning his name.

But back to the question: If you could own only *one* book on business writing, which would it be?

Well, as you might have guessed, that's not an easy question for me to answer. I feel like a kid in a candy shop with only one nickel to spend.

But if I had to limit my choice to one book, it would be Charles Brusaw, Gerald Alred, and Walter Oliu's *The Business Writers' Handbook*. This helpful, easy-to-use handbook offers excellent advice on practically all topics, large and small. Many of the entries, such as "comprise/compose" and "who's/whose," are brief, whereas others, such as "conciseness," "formal reports," and "proofreading," are developed at some length.

Every office, if not every writer, should have a copy.

What Poets Can Teach Us about Using Language

History, despite its wrenching pain,
Cannot be unlived, and if faced
With courage, need not be lived again.

—From Maya Angelou's inaugural poem,
  "On the Pulse of Morning"

"Angelou's reading may launch an era of public pride in the power of poetry," the headline read.

Maya Angelou—black, female, Southern—the first poet to read at an inauguration since James Dickey read at the New Spirit inaugural concert the night before Jimmy Carter's inauguration.

Has she in fact begun a new era? Will her example influence the way we use language? Will it change the way we think about our words?

According to Jonis Agee, professor of English and creative writing at the College of St. Catherine in St. Paul, Angelou "has elevated poetry again." In the same article, Agee was quoted as saying that young people are returning to poetry "in a response to the dominance of business and technocrat language in our culture."

"Business and technocrat language." Her phrase has stayed with me.

I know exactly what Agee has in mind. We see plenty of mindless bureaucratese, language that is devoid of human warmth or personality. And we all know about power language, language that is intended to put people in their place and to keep them there. Both types of writing hinder rather than promote genuine communication, and both do damage to the human spirit.

This is why I urge business writers to write in a natural voice. I urge them to use language that reflects their personality, to open their letters with "As you requested" rather than "As per your request" and "I am writing to let you know" rather than "The purpose of this communication is." And this is why I advocate a vocabulary based on respect and appreciation rather than one based on fear and intimidation, as in "Thank you for your fine effort" rather than "It's a good thing you met my deadline."

Still, I am troubled by the notion of dividing the world into people who speak the language of poetry and those who speak the language of "business and technocrats." It strikes me as an oversimplification. It doesn't tell the whole story.

It doesn't recognize all the good people who seek to write about technical and scientific topics in humane ways. I think of health professionals in organ procurement organizations who worry over the tone and wording of their letters as they explain to bereaved families where each organ went and how each recipient benefited. I think of William Carlos Williams and Wallace Stevens, great American poets who led double lives as a physician and insurance executive, respectively. I think of the physicist Roger Jones who explores the link between science and the creative imagination in *Physics as Metaphor* and *Physics for the Rest of Us*, and the physician Lewis Thomas who blends scientific insight with human understanding in *The Lives of the Cell*, *The Youngest Science*, and *The Fragile Species*.

Now don't get me wrong. I don't mean to suggest that, as a group, we business and technical writers don't deserve a little heat. Our readers have suffered through too many incomprehensible and insulting documents to think that there is no basis for the general resentment over "business and technocrat" language, a vocabulary that belittles a person's sense of self-worth. And I do believe that poets have something to teach us.

Poets teach us that language can go beyond clarity and overt purpose to mystery and surprise. They remind us that language can put us in touch with our common humanity. If we listen carefully, their words can lead us to the intangibles that make life worth living.

I also believe that we business writers have something to teach the poets and the academics.

We need to remind them that (to quote Angelou) ''we are more alike than we are unalike.'' We need to point out that even our pragmatic, utilitarian, hurried discourse can reflect our humanity, that the language of commerce can be something other than the language of profit, power, and privilege.

But first we must make sure we have learned these lessons ourselves.

Works Cited /
Recommended Reading

Works Cited /
Recommended Reading

American Heritage Dictionary (3rd ed., Houghton Mifflin, 1992), 6, 77

Angelou, Maya, inaugural poem, "On the Pulse of Morning," 145

Berry, Wendell, *Standing by Words* (North Point Press, 1983), 88

Brusaw, Charles, Gerald Alred, and Walter Oliu, *The Business Writers' Handbook* (4th revised ed., St. Martin's Press, 1993), 7, 144

The Chicago Manual of Style (13th ed., The University of Chicago Press, 1993), 144

Corbett, Edward P. J., *The Little English Handbook* (John Wiley & Sons, 1992), 143

Decker, Bert, *The Art of Communicating* (Crisp Publications, 1988), 87

Elbow, Peter, *Writing without Teachers* (Oxford University Press, 1973), 29, 64

Fielden, John, "What Do You Mean I Can't Write?" (*Harvard Business Review*, May-June 1964), 30

Fielden, John "What Do You Mean You Don't Like my Style?" (*Harvard Business Review*, May-June 1982), 124

Goldberg, Natalie, *Writing Down the Bones* (Shambhala, 1986), 29, 144

Gordon, Karen Elizabeth, *The Transitive Vampire: A Handbook for the Innocent, the Eager, and the Doomed* (Times Books, 1984), 60

Harper, Penny "Spellbound," 56

Jones, Roger, *Physics as Metaphor* (University of Minnesota Press, 1982), *Physics for the Rest of Us* (Contemporary Books, 1992), *146*

Kirkman, John, "How Friendly Is Your Writing for Readers Around the World?" *Text, ConText, and HyperText: Writing with and for the Computer* (MIT Press, 1988) ed. by Edward Barrett, 134

Luey, Beth, *Handbook for Academic Authors* (Cambridge University Press, 1987), 122

Maggio, Rosalie, *The Bias-Free Word Finder* (Beacon, 1992), 144

Maggio, Rosalie, *How To Say It* (Prentice Hall, 1990), 50, 107, 144

McGarvey, Robert and Scott Smith, "When Workers Rate the Boss" (*Training*, March 1993), 107

Miller, Casey, and Kate Swift, *The Handbook of Nonsexist Writing* (Harper & Row, 1988), 78, 144

Morrison, Toni, *Beloved* (Knopf, 1987), 116

Sabin, William, *The Gregg Reference Manual* (7th ed., Macmillan/McGraw-Hill, 1993), 42, 144

Schell, John, and John Stratton, *Writing on the Job* (Plume/NAL Penguin), 1984), 7

Strunk, William and E. B. White, *The Elements of Style* (Macmillan, 1959, 3rd. ed., 1979), 8, 18, 84, 85, 122, 143

Sweetnam, Sherry, *The Executive Memo* (John Wiley & Sons, 1992), 144

Tacey, William, *Business and Professional Speaking* (4th ed., Wm. C. Brown, 1983), 88

Thomas, Lewis, *The Lives of the Cell* (Viking Press, 1974), *The Youngest Science* (Viking Press, 1983), and *The Fragile Species* (Scribner's, 1992), 146

Troyka, Lynn Quitman, *Handbook for Writers* (3rd. ed., Simon & Shuster, 1992), 60

Von Diether, Barbara, "Righting Rotten Writing," (*Training*, April 1992), 34

Walker, Donald E., *The Effective Administrator* (Jossey-Bass, 1979), 93

Ward, Ritchie R., *Practical Technical Writing*, 104

Westheimer, Patricia, *The Perfect Letter* (Scott, Foresman, 1990), 122

White, E. B., *Charlotte's Web* (Harper, 1952), 143

Williams, Joseph, *Style: Ten Lessons in Clarity & Grace* (4th ed., Harper Collins College Publishers, 1994), 60, 78, 97, 143

Zinsser, William, *On Writing Well* (2nd ed., Harper & Row, 1994), 8, 78, 122, 143

Zinsser, William, *Writing with a Word Processor* (Harper & Row, 1983), 56

Index

Index

audits, wording, 109-11
block, writer's, 27-29
bureaucratese, 71-73
computers, 56-58, 59-61, 62-63, 64-66
concise writing, 17-18, 19-21
customer relations letters, 52-54
dictation, 40-42
editing, 34-36, 37-39
elegant variation, 90-92
elements of good writing, 25, 30, 84-86
errors, common, 2-3
executive summaries, 103-05
goodwill notes, 130-31
grammar checkers, programmed, 59-61
holiday greetings, 49-51
humor, 68-70, 79-81
illiteracy, 137-39
improvement plan, 5-8, 9-10, 11-12
letters of recommendation, 112-14
memos, 100-02
natural language, 14-16, 17-18, 19-21
oral presentations, preparing for, 87-89
performance reviews, 106-08, 109-11
process of writing, 24-26, 93-95
sales letters, 44-46, 47-48
score sheet, business writing, 140-42
sentence structure, variety, 119-21
simple language, 14-16, 17-18, 19-21
speech, preparing for, 87-89
spelling errors, common, 56-57
style, 116-18, 119-21, 122-23, 124-26

subordination, 120
synonyms, 90-92
thank-you notes, 128-30
that, use of, 10
translation, writing for, 134-36
variety in sentence structure, 119-21
vigorous writing (ironically presented), 74-76
wordiness, 17-18, 19-21
word processing, 56-58, 59-61, 62-63, 64-66
writer's block, 27-29
writing for translation, 134-36
writing internationally, 134-36
writing process, 24-26, 93-95